Understanding and Loving Your Child Who Smokes Pot

UNDERSTANDING AND LOVING YOUR CHILD WHO SMOKES POT

STEPHEN ARTERBURN
and MARGOT STARBUCK

SALEM
BOOKS
an imprint of Regnery Publishing
Washington, D.C.

Cataloging-in-Publication data on file with the Library of Congress

ISBN: 978-1-68451-154-9
eISBN: 978-1-68451-204-1

Library of Congress Control Number: 2021936528

Published in the United States by
Salem Books
An Imprint of Regnery Publishing
A Division of Salem Media Group
Washington, D.C.
www.SalemBooks.com

Manufactured in the United States of America

10 9 8 7 6 5 4 3 2 1

CONTENTS

CHAPTER 1
Here We Are 1

CHAPTER 2
How You Can Be the Kind of Parent Who Makes a Difference 15

CHAPTER 3
What You Need to Know about Marijuana 29

CHAPTER 4
Questions Parents Ask about Marijuana 43

CHAPTER 5
Marijuana and Family Dynamics 59

CHAPTER 6
Start Making a Difference Today 73

CHAPTER 7
Thinking through Family Policy 87

CHAPTER 8
Three Guiding Principles for Parents 99

CHAPTER 9
Implementing Family Policy 107

CHAPTER 10
When Parents Aren't on the Same Page 119

CHAPTER 11
Is There a Problem? 125

CHAPTER 12
Learning to Talk to Your Child about Marijuana 143

CHAPTER 13
Learning to Hold Space and Listen Well 157

CHAPTER 14
Get Curious, Not Furious 171

CHAPTER 15
How to Have the Conversation 179

CHAPTER 16
Engage and Stay Engaged 193

CHAPTER 17
How Not to Communicate with Your Child 201

CHAPTER 18
We're Cheering You On 209

Notes 211

CHAPTER 1

Here We Are

Patrick and Maria met as students at a small Christian college in Pennsylvania and married soon after graduation. Both had been active in their church youth groups growing up, and neither one had gotten into alcohol or drugs as teenagers. They were raising their three children—two in college and one who was a sophomore in high school.

Their youngest son, James, played baseball, and his friend group included several boys on the baseball team. Patrick and Maria didn't know those boys or their families as well as they'd known James's childhood church friends. And, like many other adolescent boys, James wasn't quite as chatty or forthcoming as he'd once been.

After James's Friday night baseball game, he climbed the bleachers to where his parents were waiting.

"Great game, kiddo," Maria said.

"Awesome hit in the second inning!" Patrick said, beaming.

"Thanks," James said with a grin. "Matt invited me to go to a sleepover with a few of the guys. That cool with you?"

"That can work," Patrick agreed. "We'll just need to be in touch with Matt's parents. They haven't left yet, so we'll go get their phone numbers while you help put equipment away."

"Cool, Dad. Thanks," James said, hopping back down and heading toward the team.

Patrick and Maria walked over to Matt's parents, and while the fathers chatted, the mothers traded phone numbers so they could stay in touch.

"If he doesn't need to get anything from home," Matt's father offered, "we can just take James home with us."

Patrick and Maria both smiled. They knew their daughter would have had to pack several bags for a sleepover but that James would be perfectly fine with just the sweaty clothes on his back.

"That sounds great," Maria said. "Thank you."

The following morning, Patrick was mowing the lawn when his phone rang. Cutting off the mower, he noticed that the number was local, but unfamiliar.

"Hello?" he answered.

"Patrick, this is Michael—Matt's father."

"Hi, Michael," Patrick replied. "Is everything alright?"

"Well..." Michael hesitated. "No one's hurt, but we do have a situation."

"I'm all ears..."

Michael explained that James and Matt and their two other friends had been in the backyard, roasting marshmallows around the fire, when he and his wife had gone to bed. The boys had promised to extinguish the fire before heading inside for the night.

"But when my wife and I were working in the yard this morning," Michael explained, "we found evidence that the boys were smoking pot last night."

Patrick, surprised, was silent.

Michael continued, "We've talked to all four boys, and they all admit that they participated. And we let them know that we'd be calling you."

"Michael, thank you," Patrick said. "This is a surprise, but we're very grateful for your call. I'll be coming by to pick up James in a few minutes, so I'll see you then."

Patrick told Maria about the phone call. They had known that some of the boys on the team smoked, but they were both genuinely surprised to learn that James had been involved. They had more questions than answers.

Was this their fault?

Were Matt's parents culpable?

Had Matt introduced James to marijuana?

Was this James's first experience, or was he using habitually?

They agreed to talk to James together, and Patrick left to pick up their son.

As he drove across town to fetch James, a thought filled his mind. *This happens to other people—not us.*

And as Maria straightened up the kitchen, she had the exact same thought: *This happens to other people—not us.*

Though neither one had consciously thought they were "inoculated" against one of their children using drugs because they'd tried to do everything "right," they realized it was what they'd each quietly believed.

Families and Marijuana

"This happens to other people—not us."

Although they'd read in the news about rising rates of teenage marijuana use, Patrick and Maria were still taken by surprise to discover their own child had used it. But because almost half of twelfth graders in the United States have used marijuana, all of us need to keep our eyes open for the possibility within our families.

Maybe you picked up this book because you are the rare parent of young children who knows you want to begin conversations about alcohol and drug use early on. (Gold star for you, Mom or Dad!)

Or maybe you are the parent of a middle schooler who's hearing rumors that other people's children are experimenting with marijuana.

You might be the parent who received a call from your child's youth pastor to let you know that your son and some friends were caught smoking marijuana during the summer service project.

Or you might be the parent of a twenty-four-year-old who is living in your basement, working a few hours a week, playing video games, and smoking pot.

Wherever you find yourself today, there can be good in store for you, for your child, and for your family.

If your children are young, we want to offer you strategies and tools to begin having conversations about marijuana before they reach middle school. If your adolescent is already experimenting with drugs, we want to equip you to help him or her by dealing squarely with the problem. And if you are parenting a child in late adolescence or young adulthood who is belligerent and unrepentant about his or her marijuana use, we believe there are steps you can take to help your child and yourself. Our aim is to help you understand and love your children.

Though we know that many parents have different views on marijuana, we believe that—with the rare medical exception—using it does not lead to human flourishing. While we acknowledge that marijuana prescribed by a thoughtful and intentional physician can have medical benefits, we believe that *recreational* marijuana use, whether it has been legalized in the state where you live or not, is detrimental to people of all ages physically, emotionally, psychologically, and even financially. We remind parents that, in every state of our nation, marijuana use for those under twenty-one remains illegal. We acknowledge that regular marijuana use for anyone under twenty-five years of age damages the developing brain. And even in states where marijuana use is legal for those over twenty-one and "less" harmful for those over twenty-five, we discourage parents from endorsing recreational marijuana use by their children in any way.

Neither of the authors of this book has ever met anyone who was smoking pot who felt like his life was really going well. None has ever reported that his career was going well, that all of his relationships were thriving, and that using marijuana was improving most of areas of his life. Despite the spin that marijuana advocates offer to justify the nationwide legalization of the drug, we believe that—with the wildly rare exception—adults and children are safer and healthier without it.

Safe and Healthy

When Margot's three children were four, five, and six years old, the question that fell off those three sweet pairs of lips, seemingly round the clock, was "Why?"

"I need you to finish your brussels sprouts, please."

"Why?"

"Please hold my hand as we're crossing the street."

"Why?"

"We're not going to watch any more television today."

"Why?"

"That's your last cookie."

"Why?"

As she answered the same question, hour after hour and day after day, she began to hear a theme in her reply. No matter what had prompted the "Why?" question, the answer she continued to parrot was usually exactly the same: "To keep you safe and healthy."

To keep you safe and healthy.

Why don't children drink alcoholic beverages? To keep them safe and healthy.

Why can't children follow that baggage handler onto the runway at the airport? To keep them safe and healthy.

Why do they have to take a nap today? To keep them safe and healthy.

As Margot heard the words cross her own lips *ad nauseum*, she began to understand more clearly her job as their mother; in part, it was to keep them safe and healthy. Physically. Socially. Emotionally. Spiritually.

Though her children are now nineteen, twenty, and twenty-one years old and are completely responsible for the choices they make, she's still navigating what it looks like to be a parent who participates in keeping her children "safe and healthy."

The challenge for many of us is how to parent faithfully in various developmental stages. Long gone are the days when some of us could simply reach up and shove a sealed bag of Oreos further into the shelf that our children couldn't reach. It's no longer sufficient to jettison what's not safe and healthy to a high shelf. As our children mature and practice greater and greater independence, our job description changes a bit.

That shift can feel difficult for many parents. But those who see clearly ultimately discover that when they can no longer "control" their children's behavior—with a tight grip while crossing the street or tossing high-carb snacks out of reach—there is still one thing they can control: themselves. You'll learn more about this in these pages.

The Teen Years

During their teen years, our children are facing several challenges. As we help them navigate the passage from childhood to adulthood, it's important to remember that. Because it's likely been a few years since we had to suffer the humiliation of changing from our school clothes into a gym uniform in front of the critical eyes of our peers, it's likely that the palpable awareness of the challenges we faced in adolescence has been mostly forgotten—not to mention that our children are dealing with things stemming from social media that were unheard of when we were their age.

The many challenges our teenage children may be facing include...

- Unconscious social pressure
- Conscious social pressure
- Romantic attraction
- A sense of identity that's in flux

- Depression
- Social anxiety
- Other anxieties
- Relationships with caregivers that might be impacted by an adult's substance use
- And so much more

During these years, our children are exploring, experimenting, and discovering who they are. They're like a cake in the oven that's not done baking! And while this can often feel more than a little precarious, it's also laden with seeds of hope. It means that stealing one of Dad's beers from the fridge or using marijuana at a sleepover doesn't signal a life sentence of deviant behavior. It means that our children are figuring out who they are—how they're like their parents and how they're different.

While none of us wants our children to have to suffer the bumps and bruises inherent in adolescence, it is a time of learning and growth that we can help them navigate.

Kids Need to Take a Break

Sixteen-year-old Leo lived with his mom and younger brother. His mother, Rebekah, had recently learned that Leo had been smoking marijuana with his friends.

Rebekah had begun talking to her boys about alcohol and drug use when they were young. And though this didn't inoculate her eldest from experimenting with marijuana, it did mean that the lines of communication were open to speak freely. In fact, when Rebekah discovered that Leo had been smoking, he said that sometimes he didn't like the way his friends behaved after they'd been using marijuana. They acted more jealous of one another when girls were around. They were moodier. Their teasing was more aggressive. And they were generally just more difficult to be around.

A few weeks before his seventeenth birthday, Leo approached Rebekah while she was doing dishes in the kitchen.

"Mom," he began, "I'm going to give up marijuana for my last year of childhood."

"Excuse me?" Rebekah asked, putting down her towel and turning to face him. "I thought we'd agreed that you were done after our last conversation."

"Sorry, Mom. My bad. But I've been thinking about it," Leo explained, "and I want to see what it would be like without the influence."

Surprised and delighted but trying to act nonchalant, Rebekah asked, "So what precipitated this?"

"Well," Leo mused, "I guess I see how it can complicate things. Friendships. Friends being touchy and moody. I didn't tell you this, but Tom gets really mean to me when he's high."

"Hmmm," Rebekah quietly reflected. "That probably doesn't feel good."

"I guess I just want to spend my last year of childhood without the complication of that."

The whole "last year of childhood" business tickled Rebekah, but she couldn't let on. She said simply, "Sure, that makes sense."

"And," Leo continued, "I'm also wondering how it'll affect my health. My digestive stuff. My soccer season. And just how I feel in general."

"Well," she answered, "you already know I'm all for it. Let me know if there's any way I can support you. I'm proud of you, babe."

Because of the climate that Rebekah had established in her home—one in which everyone was being educated, practicing awareness, taking appropriate responsibility, and exercising courage—Leo was learning how to make choices that made him safer and healthier.

Whether you're holding your toddler's hand or the hand of a grandchild, we believe that there is hope for your child who is using marijuana. Whether your engagement is preemptive or whether you're parenting in the wake of a prison sentence for drug trafficking, you can always take responsibility for yourself in a way that helps your child. Keep reading to learn how.

CHAPTER 2

How You Can Be the Kind of Parent Who Makes a Difference

Mary Jo and Paul had been divorced for four years when they began to notice that their daughter Samantha's mood and attitude toward them and her siblings had changed. She'd recently begun dating a boy from school named Trent, and they'd been spending more and more time together.

Six months earlier, when another parent had caught Samantha and her friends drinking after a school dance, Mary Jo and Paul had grounded Samantha and revoked her phone and social media privileges. Part of the consequences for her choice was that she had to give her social media passwords to her parents.

One day, Mary Jo was at work when she received a text from Paul, who'd continued to keep an eye on Samantha's social media accounts. The text chain also included Lisa, Paul's new wife. The three adults were committed to parenting Samantha together.

"I'm following a conversation Sam is having right now with someone who's selling her weed," Paul wrote.

"Wait, what?" Mary Jo replied.

Paul explained, "I still have her password for Snapchat. It's a friend of Trent's, and they're meeting him *right now* at the corner market across from the high school."

Mary Jo's brain raced to figure out how to handle the situation.

She answered, "I know she's on her way home to get her soccer cleats before practice. What should I do?"

As if it was plain as day, Paul quickly replied, "Confront them."

Mary Jo imagined confronting the pair of teens in her driveway and listening as they denied any wrongdoing. Even if she insisted on searching the car, she couldn't imagine how the scene would end successfully.

"What I don't want to do," Mary Jo texted, "is to be lied to and not find the marijuana on them."

At that moment, Mary Jo heard Trent's car rumble in to the gravel driveway.

After breezing in the back door, zipping through the kitchen, and grabbing her cleats from the mudroom, Samantha offered a quick, "Hi, Mom! Bye, Mom!" before shutting the back door and returning to Trent's car.

Dizzied and unsure of the best course of action, Mary Jo heard the pair leave. What to do in a situation that would have seemed so cut and dried if her neighbor had shared it with her on a morning walk felt confusing and overwhelming in the moment.

"Well," she reported on the text thread, feeling as though she'd failed, "she just came and went. So what's next?"

Paul's wife Lisa, who hadn't yet chimed in, gently offered, "I just don't feel good about her driving with someone who might be under the influence."

Of course. The soft words were the smack in the face Mary Jo needed. Of course! Rather than dwell in regret, she sprang into action.

Dialing her daughter's phone, she waited for Samantha to pick up.

"Hey, Mom," Samantha answered brightly, in a pleasant tone that had become atypical for the teen. "Whuzzup?"

"Sam," her mother announced calmly, "you're not going to soccer practice today. Please have Trent bring you home right now."

"What?" Sam asked indignantly. "Why?"

"Your dad and Lisa and I know that you just bought marijuana," she said patiently. "I need you to come home right now and bring it with you."

"What are you talking about?" Sam asked, her tone sounding like a desperate animal caught in a cage.

Mary Jo had experienced her daughter's tenacious denials before, and today she wasn't having it. She also wasn't going to let on how the parenting trio had come by the information.

"Sam," she said sternly, "come home now. Bring the marijuana."

Seeing no way out, Sam backpedaled, "Mom, it isn't even ours. It's for someone else—I promise."

Sam had little awareness of how little her promises had come to mean.

"Now," her mother reiterated. "And bring what you bought."

"Whatever," Sam huffed, hanging up the phone.

Five minutes later, Mary Jo heard the car in the driveway again. Dragging herself through the back door, eyes down, Sam dropped a small baggie of marijuana on the kitchen counter.

"Phone, too," her mother instructed.

Without a word, Sam dropped her phone and marched through the house toward her bedroom.

Before going to speak with her daughter, Mary Jo texted Paul and Lisa. "Sam's at home. We'll talk more later. Lisa, thank you."

In a sudden situation that felt overwhelming, her ex-husband's new wife had reminded Mary Jo of one of the prime parenting directives: protect your child.

Parental Ambivalence

We see far too many parents today who feel caught in the bind in which Paul and Mary Jo found themselves. They recognize a problem, but they're hesitant to do what needs to be done when it needs to be done.

Jim Burns and Stephen Arterburn cowrote *How to Talk to Your Kids about Drugs* (formerly titled *Drug-Proofing Your Child*) because they were convinced that parents can protect children when they take action. But of course, not all parents are taking action. And according to the authors, there are four reasons why.

The first reason why parents fail to make a difference is ignorance. Even those who agree that marijuana use is a problem in our country can easily fool themselves into thinking it's not in their town, not in their high school, and not in their home. Choosing to remain ignorant not only blinds us to the problem, but also prevents us from being a part of the solution.

The second reason why parents fail to make a difference is denial. We refuse to face our child's condition because we're unwilling to experience the temporary pain that comes when choosing to intervene for the good of another. If we deny what's happening, we don't have to deal with the problem.

A third reason why parents aren't making a difference is guilt. It's easy for parents to blame themselves when something goes wrong with their children. They might also feel guilty if they're abusing substances themselves. But when they're paralyzed by guilt, they can't make the tough decisions necessary to serve their children.

A final reason why parents don't engage effectively is fear. Some fear being rejected by their children. Some fear the unknown of what life might look like after the child changes. And others fear doing the wrong thing, possibly exacerbating the problem. Yet if they're going to help their kids, they need to move toward action.

We suspect that one or all of these resonate with you in some way. But rather than feeling burdened by these natural temptations, why don't we flip them and look at the strengths you will need for this journey toward health?

How You Can Make a Difference

As we journey together in this book, we want to reinforce the same four principles that make a difference in the life of your child when it comes to drug prevention, drug use, and drug recovery.

Education

First, we want you to educate yourself. We'll share some of the basics you need to know about marijuana and also answers to questions a lot of parents like you are asking. When you reject ignorance, you choose education. Learn all you can about teen marijuana use and continue to seek out the best information.

Awareness

In addition to education, we encourage you to commit to becoming more *aware*. We know how tempting it can be to keep our blinders on, but when you reject denial, you can finally embrace awareness. Refuse to shut your eyes to the signs—subtle and overt—that your child needs help. Stay vigilant.

Appropriate Responsibility

Thirdly, we want to educate and equip you to take appropriate responsibility for the choices your child makes about drugs. In some cases, that will mean you'll accept responsibility for the role you might have played, or are currently playing, in the choices your child is making. And in other cases, accepting appropriate responsibility means you will reject guilt and shame that is not yours. When you reject guilt, you embrace appropriate responsibility. Rejecting guilt doesn't mean you're completely innocent! But when you accept appropriate responsibility, you refuse to stay stuck in guilt.

Courage

And finally, we encourage you to practice courage in your parenting. We understand the fears you're facing, but when you reject fear, you embrace courage. Commit to bravely confronting the problem and seeking solutions. Know and trust that there is One who will meet your needs in every moment.

Does Any of This Feel Familiar?

We can relate to what Mary Jo, Paul, and Lisa faced as parents who discovered their child on the cusp of adulthood had been using marijuana. And the twisty logic with which we, and many other parents, were afflicted sounded something like this:

If he's under eighteen, I can't throw him out on the street. So I have to put up with this behavior.

If he's over eighteen, he's technically an adult and is making his own choices. So I have to put up with this behavior.

If you've felt stuck in that thought process, we understand. We know that when parents first learn of their child's experimentation with drugs, we can quickly spiral into thoughts of our beloved babies living in an alley under a cardboard box. And that fear of what might happen to our loved ones can paralyze us and keep us from taking action. It can be hard to see clearly.

Steve has remarked that parents' biggest hesitation for implementing predetermined consequences is the accusatory voice in our heads that says, "You can't throw her out on the street!" And that's actually fair. Steve notes, "If you throw them out on the street, they might get hit by a car. The driveway or front yard is far enough."

When your child is living at home, you have something they want: food and shelter. And to allow them to use drugs while they're living in your home enables them, encourages them, and perpetuates the problem. Margot learned that from Steve, and it was a critical insight that helped her. A friend who was helping her think through how to respond echoed that wisdom by telling her bluntly, "*Your* house, *your* rules." While it felt cold, something about this insight felt very right! (Her friend also offered to send her a tent that her child could use for shelter when he was living in the driveway.)

For so many years, her home had been a "nest" where her baby birds were protected and nurtured, first by two parents and then by one on-site and one off-site. It was the one place in the world where they were always loved. Always accepted. Always received. So it was a challenge for Margot to shift the way she thought about her home. And truthfully, she didn't *want* to assume a posture that felt very cold to her: *my house, my rules*. She also suspected that establishing those firm boundaries would be a bit more difficult as a single parent than it would have been if she'd had a partner.

As parents who purpose to pattern our lives after Christ, many of us have embraced a self-emptying posture toward our children. The sacrifices we make—leaving work early to attend soccer games, missing an event at church to care for a sick child, or foregoing purchases we might enjoy—don't feel like sacrifices at all. Both biological and adopted, these little (and not so little) people are bone of our bone and flesh of our flesh. We would do anything for them, wouldn't we?

So the shift Margot had to make in her head was that "my house, my rules" actually was loving and serving her child. The rules she'd established for her home—curfew, quiet hours after 11:00 p.m., a parent needs to be home if friends are over, no occupants using illicit drugs—were in place *for the sake of* her children. She had to reframe her thinking to agree with the reality that saying "my rules" was not self-serving but was in service to her child.

It took some time to wrap her mind around that one. The nagging voice of the enemy badgered, "What kind of parent kicks their child out on the street? What kind of monster are you?" And in the midst of the madness, the voice of truth reminded her, "You are not the offender here. Your child is making these choices. Establishing clear, healthy boundaries is the most loving way forward."

Would people look at her sideways when they heard she'd kicked her child out of the home? Maybe. But hoping the problem would go away on its own wasn't working.

Stay in the Game

After Sandy and John discovered their son Josh was vaping marijuana, they committed themselves to staying in conversation with him about it. They sent him articles about how marijuana affects the brain. They shared YouTube videos of celebrities who'd chosen to leave marijuana behind. And they even arranged a conversation between Josh and a family friend who was a psychiatrist to help him better understand the potential impact of the choices he was making. They were strategic about how often they brought it up, but they didn't back off because of some grumbling or an eye roll.

Sometimes their intervention would be formal; they'd pull up a video to watch together after dinner. Other times it was more casual. When John picked up Josh after a party with the other members of his baseball team and smelled Josh's clothes, he initiated a conversation by blurting "Man, what's up?" instead of ignoring it or waiting until a "better" time. He and Sandy would occasionally remind Josh, "Don't drive with anyone who's been using. If you call us for a ride, you won't get in trouble." While they didn't hammer on marijuana use day and night, they were consistent in communicating with their son.

Their efforts, as many of ours can be, were hit and miss. Josh didn't read most of the articles they shared, but he did get invested in watching some of the YouTube videos. And in surprising moments when John or Sandy would bring up the issue, the family had some good exchanges.

Sandy now counsels other parents, "Be vigilant. Put on your sleuth hat. Notice the patterns."

What Sandy and John *did right* was to stay in the game. It would have been easier to sit their son down, have one difficult conversation, and then move on. But they were committed to keeping the lines of communication open with their son.

You Can Do This

We expect that you've met some parents who are hesitant to do what needs to be done when it needs to be done too. Maybe they're afraid that enforcing consequences that will be effective will drive their children further away from them. Or maybe they've convinced themselves that their children's marijuana use really isn't that big of a problem. Maybe they've gone so far as to *allow* marijuana use under the "safety" of their roof. Or maybe they've just given up because they don't feel like there's anything they can do.

We believe you can make a difference in your child's life, and we're eager to equip you to do that. When you educate yourself, commit to staying aware, shoulder appropriate responsibility, and exercise the courage God grants you, you can better understand and love your child who is using marijuana.

CHAPTER 3

What You Need to Know about Marijuana

When you hear the word "marijuana," what connotations does it evoke for you? If you're the parent of a teen or young adult today, chances are good that the word conjures up different images for you than it might for your child. If you were a teen in the seventies or eighties, you might think of the "potheads" or "burnouts" who regularly used the illicit drug. But today, marijuana use among young people spans every social group, including star athletes, honor roll students, and even church kids.

By the time they've reached twelfth grade, 43.7 percent of teens have used marijuana. Over one-third have used it in the previous year, and more than one-fifth have used it in the previous month.[1] Clearly, marijuana use is no longer relegated to an alternative subculture within a high school. In fact, daily marijuana use by teens in eighth, ninth, and tenth grade has risen significantly over the last few years. While 6.4 percent of twelfth graders use marijuana daily, 4.8 percent of tenth traders admit to daily use.[2]

We want you to know the basics about marijuana so that you'll have resources for conversations in your home. There's a lot of misinformation out there, and you can best understand and love your child when you have the most reliable information about marijuana.

Cannabis

Marijuana is made from the leaves and dried flowers of the cannabis plant. The compounds in cannabis that can produce a variety of physiological effects are called phytocannabinoids. The plant contains over a hundred different cannabinoids, and when they are received by the cannabinoid receptors found throughout the body, they are transported to the brain. The two cannabinoids that are important for you to understand are Tetrahydrocannabinol (THC) and Cannabidiol (CBD).

Many assume that THC is the "fun" or "recreational" agent in marijuana and CBD is the "medicinal" part. It's true that THC is responsible for the "high" feeling many get when using marijuana. And it's also true that CBD, often used for medical therapies, is non-intoxicating. While research has shown that CBD can lower anxiety, reduce cravings, and help with moods, making it technically a psychoactive substance, it doesn't make a user "high." Marijuana in various forms—as well as other products derived from the cannabis plant—have varying concentrations of THC and CBD.

It's natural for parents who live in states that have not legalized recreational marijuana to be baffled when they see shops selling CBD products or even notice candies displayed at the gas station cash register that contain CBD. It can be very confusing! While CBD from marijuana is not federally legal, legislation passed in 2018 called the Hemp Farming Act, which allows the cultivation of hemp plants, made CBD legal if it's derived from hemp and contains less that 0.3 percent THC. This is why, even if marijuana isn't legal in your state, you'll see products that contain CBD at stores and even gas stations near you.

Being able to see a bit of marijuana's history in our country can help you see where we are today by showing you where we've been.

Federal Law and State Laws

The federal government began regulating the sale and use of marijuana with the passage of the Marihuana Tax Act of

1937. Then in 1970, the Controlled Substances Act classified cannabis as a Schedule 1 drug (which includes those that have been determined to have a high potential for abuse and no accepted medical use). Though both of those claims are disputed by many today, marijuana remains a federally classified Schedule 1 drug.

In recent years, however, various states have legalized marijuana for medical use and/or recreational use. By the beginning of 2021, thirty-four states had legalized the use of marijuana for medical purposes, and eleven states had legalized recreational marijuana. (If you're wondering what the laws are in your state, visit the Marijuana Policy Project's page at www.mpp.org/states.)

For example, Margot lives in North Carolina, where recreational use is not legal, but the North Carolina Compassionate Use Registration Act of 2014 allows patients with intractable epilepsy to access low-THC hemp extract as an alternative form of treatment. And Indiana, where Steve lives, has some of the strictest marijuana laws in the nation: recreational marijuana use is illegal, and there are no provisions for medical marijuana use.

But in California, state laws are much more liberal. In 1996, California became the first state to legalize medical cannabis and then legalized the use of recreational cannabis in 2016. This means that any adult over twenty-one can purchase marijuana for personal use there.

This patchwork of state and federal statutes can be confusing. How can states be legalizing a substance that is *federally* illegal? Because in 2014, the passage of the Rohrabacher-Farr amendment prohibited the U.S. Justice Department from interfering with the implementation of state *medical* cannabis laws.

But transporting cannabis between states, even when it is legal on both ends of the trip, remains a federal crime because the U.S. Constitution gives the federal government the right to control and regulate commerce between states. Practically, this means that if someone from Indiana goes on vacation in California and decides to buy a chocolate bar containing marijuana, they cannot legally take it back to Fort Wayne. In some states where marijuana is illegal that are adjacent to states where marijuana is legal, troopers are waiting to catch those trying to smuggle it in.

Marijuana Hasn't Always Been Illegal

Although marijuana is currently classified as a Schedule 1 substance, it hasn't always been considered dangerous. In the nineteenth century and into the twentieth, cannabis was widely accepted as a therapeutic treatment throughout North America. Opiates and cocaine were also largely unregulated.

In fact, in the 1890s, the Sears and Roebuck catalogue sold a syringe with a small amount of cocaine in it.[3]

Restrictions making marijuana illegal began occurring in the United States during the early twentieth century for reasons as arguably political as they were medical. The fact is that restricting marijuana use is relatively *new* in human history. Evidence shows that cannabis was farmed as many as six thousand years ago, and the earliest record of its being used for medicinal purposes was in China in 2737 BC.[4] Over the centuries and across a variety of cultures, cannabis has been used to treat everything from tumors to lisps to constipation to hair loss. In fact, the National Institutes of Health (NIH) reports "cannabis was widely utilized as a patent medicine during the 19th and early 20th centuries, described in the United States Pharmacopoeia for the first time in 1850."[5]

As you weigh the dangers and benefits of marijuana, it's important to distinguish between recreational and medical use.

Recreational Marijuana

In the eleven states where marijuana has been legalized for recreational use, any adult over twenty-one can buy it. (What we're calling "recreational use" is also referred to as "adult use.")

Because recreational marijuana use is not supervised by a physician, there are certain inherent risks. For example, where recreational use has been legalized, most—*but not all*—states require that products purchased from a licensed facility must be tested by a state-accredited laboratory to ensure safety. This testing should identify the ratios of THC to CBD present, as well as the presence of pesticides and other contaminants, mold and mildew, heavy metals, and other foreign materials. But the reality is that the quality and thoroughness of testing varies from state to state.

That being the case, you can only imagine that in states where marijuana is being sold on the streets—which, of course, is every state—there is no regulatory process ensuring the safety of these products. Without lab testing, there is simply no way of knowing what these products contain.

This means that the student or creepy adult who sells weed to teens can tell them anything they want, but there's no way to know what kinds of contaminants are in it.

Medical Marijuana

Though this book is not intended to deal with the many issues around the use of medical marijuana, we want to include a bit of information to help you understand the differences between recreational marijuana use and medical use.

As a parent, you're likely trying to discern how "bad" or "good" marijuana actually is. That's a complicated question. The father or mother of a sixteen-year-old boy who smokes marijuana regularly and begins to lose his motivation to do well in school and at work is keenly aware of the negative effects of marijuana. But what about the other potential uses of cannabis? Is there anything helpful about it for anyone?

A girl named Charlotte Figi, born in 2006, was three months old when she had her first seizure. By the time she was five, she was suffering up to three hundred grand mal seizures a week as a result of Dravet syndrome—a condition seen typically during the first year of life which causes frequent febrile seizures that can be life-threatening. In 2012, Charlotte's mother, Paige, offered her daughter CBD oil derived from the marijuana plant. The family saw an immediate reduction in Charlotte's symptoms as her seizures dropped from three hundred a week down to just two or three per month. Families of other suffering children began moving to Colorado to access the same kind of help. Charlotte's story began to spread beyond the Dravet syndrome community when it was featured in a 2013 documentary by CNN medical correspondent Sanjay Gupta.

Charlotte's story, like those of many other children, makes many of the questions around the "badness" or "goodness" of marijuana much more nuanced. We recognize that there are medical benefits that can be derived from the marijuana plant, and we also emphasize to parents and families that "recreational" use of marijuana is very different than its "medical" use, which is supervised by doctors.

Of the thirty-four states that had approved marijuana for medical use as of 2020, each has identified specific conditions that can be treated with medical marijuana. You'll remember that in North Carolina, only intractable seizures related to epilepsy are eligible for treatment with medical marijuana. However, many more conditions qualify to receive recommendations for medical marijuana in New York, including:

> cancer, HIV infection or AIDS, amyotrophic lateral sclerosis (ALS), Parkinson's disease, multiple sclerosis, spinal cord injury with spasticity, epilepsy, inflammatory bowel disease, neuropathy, Huntington's disease, post-traumatic stress disorder or chronic pain...or any condition for which an opioid could be prescribed.... The severe debilitating or life-threatening condition must also be accompanied by one or more of the following associated or complicating conditions: cachexia or wasting syndrome, severe or chronic pain, severe nausea, seizures, or

> severe persistent muscle spasms, PTSD or opioid use disorder....[6]

The way that marijuana helps these various medical conditions varies. For instance, it may provide relief for a woman enduring grueling chemotherapy treatments for breast cancer, alleviating nausea and vomiting. Like the benefit it offers to those suffering from intractable seizures, marijuana can provide relief to spasticity due to injury, multiple sclerosis, and other afflictions. It can also benefit those suffering from PTSD, allowing many debilitated by the condition to return to normal living. It has even been shown to help those addicted to opioids overcome the dangerous addiction.[7] For those who suffer, I am grateful that the cannabis plant can bring relief.

There may be more medical benefits that can be gleaned from it, but here's the rub: Since marijuana has been a controlled substance since 1937 and classified as a Schedule 1 substance since 1970, there has not been a lot of modern research conducted on it. We mention this as a reminder that the larger conversation about the harmfulness and helpfulness of marijuana is nuanced.

We're also keenly aware that your attention is not on the medical benefits of marijuana if you're the parent of someone who is using marijuana recreationally. But it's helpful to understand how and why one medication made from the cannabis plant and several that are synthetic are helping those who suffer.

Medications Approved by the Federal Government

Getting cannabis-based medications approved by the federal government is tricky. The fact that cannabis is federally illegal means that researchers can't readily study it. There have been some authorized exceptions, but as more states legalize marijuana, we need much more research to understand its short- and long-term impacts on the human body.

To date, four medications containing cannabis have been approved by the Food and Drug Administration.

In 1985, Marinol was approved for the treatment of nausea and vomiting associated with chemotherapy treatments for cancer. In 1992, the same drug was approved to be used to treat dangerous weight loss in patients with AIDS. Rather than using extracts from the cannabis plant, Marinol is actually produced synthetically in a laboratory.

A second synthetic drug containing THC, Cesamet, was approved in 2006 to treat the nausea and vomiting associated with cancer treatments.

Syndros, also a synthetic drug containing a THC formulation, was also approved to treat these symptoms.

Most recently, a fourth drug, Epidiolex, was approved in 2018 for the treatment of two rare seizure disorders in children over the age of two. One of those is Lennox-Gastaut, and the other is Dravet syndrome, which is what Charlotte Figi lived with. Lennox-Gastaut begins when children are three to five years of age and causes brutal seizures with uncontrolled muscle contractions.

Charlotte Figi died in the spring of 2020 at the age of thirteen, but her story has been instrumental in the legalization of medical marijuana in the United States, such as the 2018 approval of Epidiolex. What makes Epidiolex different than the previous FDA-approved drugs containing cannabinoids is that rather than being synthetically fabricated, it contains CBD extracted directly from the cannabis plant.

Methods of Delivery

Those of us old enough to have children who are teens and young adults might not be familiar with the various methods of ingesting marijuana. Once upon a time, users "smoked joints" and "ate edibles." While these methods of consumption are both available today, there are a number of other ways marijuana can enter the body.

According to many popular cultural stereotypes, marijuana can be consumed in the form of a rolled joint, with dried marijuana leaves being rolled into paper and smoked like a cigar. Marijuana can also be smoked through a pipe. Both methods deliver the drug through the lungs, into the blood system, and to the brain. As a result, the effects of marijuana can be felt more quickly. One increased risk of this method, however, is that smoking can damage the lungs.

Like the legendary "pot brownies" many of us heard of in the 1970s, 1980s, and 1990s, marijuana can be included as an active ingredient in a variety of foods. While this is a slower method of delivery, since it requires metabolization in the gastrointestinal tract, it can have a longer-lasting effect than other methods.

Another popular way of consuming marijuana these days is vaping: A device heats an oil-based mixture that is inhaled by the user. Like smoking, the effects from vaping are felt immediately. And like smoking, vaping also puts the user's lungs at risk.

Marijuana can also be consumed orally in a capsule form. Like edibles, the effects take longer to experience but will likely be longer-lasting. Because it bypasses the lungs, this method is considered safer for those with respiratory issues or lung disease.

Another way the body can absorb cannabis products is by applying oils to the skin in the forms of creams or lotions. They can also be absorbed when they are part of a tincture, a concentrated liquid that can be placed beneath the tongue.

If your child is getting high from marijuana, though, he or she is likely not lathering up with lotion. He or she is most likely either smoking, vaping, or consuming edibles.

CHAPTER 4

Questions Parents Ask about Marijuana

Jennifer was working from home and her husband was traveling when she received a call on her cell phone that she recognized as the number of her son's school.

"Hello," she answered.

"Hey, Mom, I need you to come to school," her son Terry said. Jennifer could hear noise from the school's main office in the background.

"Babe," Jennifer asked with concern, "are you okay?"

"Yeah, I'm good," he said. "You just need to talk to the vice principal."

Jennifer's concern for her son's safety was replaced by concern about his behavior.

"About what?" she asked.

Lowering his voice, Terry said, "I can tell you more when you get here. A teacher found something in my backpack, but it's not even mine."

Nothing about her son's denial rang true.

Glancing at the clock, Jennifer agreed. "I have a Zoom meeting at four, but I can come now if it's quick."

"Thanks, Mom."

Fifteen minutes later, when Jennifer arrived in the school office, her son rose to meet her. The vice principal had stepped out, giving them a few minutes alone together in the main office.

"Mom," Terry whispered, "it's not even mine. This girl asked me to hold this stuff for her, and I didn't know what to do—"

The vice principal walked into the room and signaled them to join him in his private office. Following him, they exchanged greetings and sat down.

"Thanks for coming, Mrs. Harrison," Mr. Smith said. "Mr. Rowe overheard some kids in the hallway, and when he asked Terry to open his backpack, he found these."

Mr. Smith showed Jennifer some items that could have been candy dispensers. She deduced they were not.

Reading her face, Mr. Smith said, "These are vaping devices. And we also found some tobacco JUULpods. So Terry will have detention for all of next week."

Jennifer nodded.

"If we'd found marijuana," he explained, "we would have had to suspend him from school."

"Of course," Jennifer agreed.

Terry looked down at the ground.

Turning to him, Mr. Smith said, "You can go back to seventh period. And I don't want to see you in here again, Terry."

"Yes, sir," Terry said, turning to return to class.

"T," his mom called after him, "we'll talk about this tonight when your dad gets home." Then, turning to Mr. Smith, she said, "I'm so sorry about this. We really had no idea."

Mr. Smith answered, "Terry's a good kid. We're just seeing an awful lot of this. Thanks for coming in."

As she walked back to her car, Jennifer's mind raced. What was vaping, anyway? Was it something other than marijuana? Was it legal or illegal? Was vaping a gateway to harder drugs?

She just didn't know.

Questions Many Parents Have about Marijuana

Is Marijuana Harmful?

Those who advocate for recreational marijuana use insist that it isn't harmful. There are various reasons they might say this: They might reason that a "high" from marijuana isn't debilitating in the way that some harder drugs might be. They may be thinking of marijuana strains from thirty or forty years ago that were less potent than they are today. But no matter what logic is offered, the fact remains that regular marijuana use is harmful.

- Like tobacco, marijuana contains cancer-causing agents.
- Marijuana harms the brain.
- Marijuana strains the cardiovascular system, raising the heart rate by as much as 50 percent.
- Marijuana harms short-term memory retention and the ability to concentrate.
- Chronic marijuana use can lead to "amotivational syndrome" that includes lethargy, reduced attention span, and general lack of interest in anything other than getting high.
- Marijuana reduces the division of disease-repelling white blood cells, diminishing the body's ability to protect itself from illnesses.
- Marijuana may cause users to experience acute panic and anxiety.

While some of these effects aren't immediately evident, they are nonetheless real and measurable.

Is Marijuana Addictive?

Marijuana is not addictive in the same ways that hard drugs can be, though its uses can be problematic. The Diagnostic and Statistical Manual of Mental Disorders (DSM-5) identifies cannabis use disorder by defining nine pathological patterns classified under impaired control, social impairment, risky behavior, or physiological adaptions.[1] A study in *JAMA Psychiatry* reveals that 30 percent of those who use marijuana may have some degree of this disorder.[2] Also, those who begin using marijuana before the age of eighteen are four to seven times more likely to develop the disorder in adulthood than others.

How Do I Know If My Child Is Addicted to Marijuana?

The DSM-5 notes the following criteria for recognizing cannabis use disorder:

- Taking more cannabis than was intended
- Difficulty controlling or cutting down cannabis use
- Spending a lot of time on cannabis use
- Craving cannabis
- Problems at work, school, and home as a result of cannabis use

- Continuing to use cannabis despite social or relationship problems
- Giving up or reducing other activities in favor of cannabis
- Taking cannabis in high-risk situations
- Continuing to use cannabis despite physical or psychological problems
- Developing a tolerance for cannabis
- Withdrawal when discontinuing cannabis[3]

If you recognize any of these symptoms in your child, it's time to get help.

How Might Marijuana Harm My Teen or Young Adult Child?

While we recognize the proven and potential benefits of medical marijuana, we are extremely concerned about the harm that recreational marijuana can do to individuals—especially young people. Teens and young adults are particularly vulnerable since the brain continues to develop from the prenatal stage into the mid-twenties. The harm suffered before the brain is fully developed has lifelong effects, many of which we are still discovering.

Recently, a study evaluated more than 62,000 human brains using a SPECT scan (Single Photon Emission Computed Tomography), which evaluates blood flow in different regions of the brain. Reduced blood flow can indicate disease or disorder. The researchers examined 128 regions of the brain to predict the chronological age of the patient, and they found that certain behaviors could predict aging; cannabis abuse accelerated brain aging by 2.8 years. In light of these results, Dr. Daniel Amen, a psychiatrist recognized as one of America's leading brain health experts and the founder of a nationwide chain of clinics that bears his name, said, "The cannabis abuse finding was especially important, as our culture is starting to see marijuana as an innocuous substance. This study should give us pause about it."[4]

The U.S. Surgeon General's Advisory on marijuana warned that frequent use during adolescence was associated with the following:

- Changes in the area of the brain involved in attention, memory, decision-making, and motivation. Deficits in attention and memory have been detected in marijuana-using teens even after a month of abstinence.

- Impaired learning in adolescents. Chronic use is linked to declines in IQ, school performance that jeopardizes professional and social achievements, and life satisfaction.
- Increased school absences and drop-out rates, as well as suicide attempts.
- Risk for and early onset of psychotic disorders, such as schizophrenia. The risk for psychotic disorders increases with frequency of use, potency of the marijuana product, and as the age of first use decreases.
- Other substance use. In 2017, teens between the ages of twelve and seventeen reporting frequent use of marijuana showed a 130 percent greater likelihood of misusing opioids.[5]

These are the consequences of marijuana use of which we're currently aware. But due to current limitations on research, there is much more to be learned about the impact of marijuana on the developing brain.

It's worth noting that many doctors who are licensed to certify medical marijuana will avoid recommending vape pens and joints because of potential harm to the lungs—the same kinds of difficulties that are related to tobacco use.

If the Risks of Marijuana Use Are Documented, Why Do People Say It Is Harmless?

The likely reason that many continue to insist that marijuana is harmless is because, unlike drugs such as heroin, methamphetamine, or cocaine, people aren't dying from marijuana overdoses. While medically true, this logic neglects the other physical, emotional, and relational consequences of marijuana use.

Does Marijuana Use Decrease Motivation?

If you're wondering whether marijuana decreases motivation in teens, you're not alone. As far back as 1894, the Indian Hemp Drugs Commission reported that heavy cannabis use was associated with apathy.[6] And in 1968, UCLA's Louis Jolyon West and William H. McGlothlin published *The Marihuana Problem: An Overview*, in which they identified what they called "Cannabis amotivational syndrome" as "apathy and diminished ability to concentrate, follow routines, or successfully master new material."[7]

Most experts today, however, would concur that we don't have the research to say definitively that the apathy seen in marijuana users is medical (the brain tissue has changed) or behavioral (the person is making getting and using marijuana his or her priority.)

Parent, you know your child. Trust your instincts.

Does Marijuana Affect Mental Health?

Researchers at King's College London discovered that daily marijuana users were three times more likely to be diagnosed with psychosis—and those who used high-potency marijuana daily were five times more likely to develop it.[8] What's particularly concerning is that researchers are not able to predict who will be impacted in this way. While there's much more we need to learn about marijuana and why people react differently to it, we do know statistically that marijuana use increases the likelihood of developing psychosis.

Is Marijuana Different Today Than When I Was Young?

When Steve was in middle school and high school in the late 1960s, marijuana advocates claimed it wasn't harmful. They insisted it was less dangerous than alcohol because users didn't experience hangovers. It's important to us that you hear this: Today's marijuana isn't the same as what was available when you were young. If you are parenting teens or young adults today, it's fair to say that the marijuana your child might consume is likely to be different than the marijuana of your youth.

In an essay published in the *New Yorker* in 2019, journalist Malcolm Gladwell wrote, "Because of recent developments in plant breeding and growing techniques, the typical concentration of THC, the psychoactive ingredient in marijuana, has gone from the low single digits to more than twenty per cent—from a swig of near-beer to a tequila shot."[9] Charas Scientific, a Colorado laboratory that tests cannabis, confirms that today the THC content in marijuana is typically between 18 and 30 percent—two to three times as potent as marijuana that was grown, sold, and consumed in the 1980s.[10] And unless marijuana has undergone third-party testing, it's impossible to know what its potency actually is.

How Will Marijuana Make My Child Feel?

Janelle has three children who are now all young adults. Each tried marijuana in high school or college. Janelle's oldest child reported that smoking marijuana didn't have much of an effect on him at all; he didn't notice any psychotropic effects. But when her daughter tried vaping marijuana, she felt nauseous and sick to her stomach. She also felt anxious and paranoid. When Janelle's younger daughter was in college, she ate some cookies that had been laced with marijuana and began to experience some of the common effects people who use marijuana report, such as feeling peaceful and happy, having an altered sense of time and space, and noticing an increased appetite.

There are several reasons why each of Janelle's children might have experienced marijuana differently:

- Simply put, different people experience the same drug in different ways because everyone's biology is unique. And it's not possible to predict how someone will or will not react.
- It's possible to smoke or vape without inhaling deeply into the lungs.
- All three children likely consumed different quantities of marijuana at different rates.
- Because these drugs were obtained on the street, there is no way of knowing the amount of CBD or THC that each contained.
- Because it can take longer to feel the effects of edibles, individuals might consume much more of the drug than they realize because it's slow-acting.

So while different marijuana users report different symptoms, there are some common effects people may experience:

- Heightened senses, where lights, sounds, and colors may feel particularly intense
- Feeling less inhibited, becoming more talkative than usual, or behaving uncharacteristically
- Distortion of time, distance, or space, perhaps not realizing time has passed
- A sense of relaxation, lightheartedness, and low anxiety
- A greater sense of profundity, as if the user's observations are more meaningful than they really are
- Increase in appetite
- Finding things funny that may or may not be humorous

So What Is Vaping, Anyway?

Today, more young people are vaping than smoking cigarettes. Vaping devices, also known as e-cigarettes, are battery-operated devices used to inhale an aerosol, typically containing nicotine—though some teens, drawn to the fruity flavors, don't even realize that is present. Marijuana can also be vaped when the products contain THC. Because vaping is a more potent delivery system, users will feel more high from vaping than from smoking.

While e-cigarettes do expose users to fewer toxic chemicals than regular cigarettes, they are still dangerous; inhaling smoke of any kind is bad for lung health.

Should I Be Testing My Child for Marijuana?

There isn't a one-size-fits-all answer to this question.

If your child experimented with marijuana, got sick, and has zero interest in trying it again, you likely don't need to implement regular drug testing. However, if your child is failing in school, has a chronic habit of lying, and wants to keep using marijuana, he or she would likely be well-served both by regular drug testing and the gift of a counselor to whom he or she can speak on a regular basis.

A good rule of thumb is to trust that your child is telling you the truth until you can't. If your child "stretches the truth" or is dishonest about other things, it's fair to assume that he or she may also be lying about marijuana.

How Do I Test My Child for Marijuana?

Most drugstores today carry drug-testing kits. The ones that test just for marijuana cost about twenty dollars, and kits that test for more drugs will be more expensive. The kit contains a plastic cup, like you get at the doctor's office, to collect urine and a strip that you will dip into the urine that will indicate whether marijuana is present. The window of time that marijuana will show up in urine after using it depends on frequency and the amount that has been ingested. Urine tests detect marijuana for anywhere from three to thirty days after use.[11]

How Do I Know If My Child Needs Professional Help?

It depends on how old your child is.

For instance, if your child is seventeen and you discover that he's been using marijuana regularly for several years, you don't have time to mess around. You want to do everything you can while that child is still living with you—especially if his choices suggest that he won't have the privilege of living with you for long! After your child turns eighteen, you won't have the ability to help him in the same ways you can when he's underage. If your child is struggling with marijuana use at sixteen or seventeen, we suggest that you do *more* rather than less. You can choose between outpatient therapy or an inpatient treatment program, but please be aware that the clock is ticking.

If your child is thirteen or fourteen, you have a little more wiggle room to try various options.

And if your child is older than eighteen, you can recommend that he or she gets professional help, but the decision ultimately will be his or hers. At this age, you can't control your child's choices—if you ever could!—but you can control the way you enable or respond to those choices.

CHAPTER 5

Marijuana and Family Dynamics

Jim and Deborah, parents of four children between the ages of ten and twenty, had been married for twenty-two years. Their family members were actively involved in youth sports, committed members of their church, and volunteered in the community. From the outside, they appeared to have it all.

Not long after their wedding anniversary, Jim came home from a business trip and announced to his wife that he was leaving her. He'd been having an affair and was expecting a child with a woman in another state. Deborah was stunned. Despite the seismic shift, Deborah and Jim did remain united in wanting to love and support their children.

After a few months of counseling together, the couple gathered their children to share that their marriage was ending and that Jim would be moving to another state to be with another woman and their new child. After a good deal of silence, the couple's oldest son said he still loved his dad. Their sixteen-year-old twin girls asked a few questions. Their youngest was silent. Both Deborah and Jim affirmed that they loved their children and would continue to work together to care for them.

The weeks and months following that family meeting went as well as could be expected. Jim would often do a FaceTime call with the family for dinner where conversations about the high school soccer coach, the youth group ski trip, and summer job applications continued as they always had. Deborah's robust network of friends cared for her, brought by the occasional meal, and helped with the kids' busy transportation schedules. Deborah visited with her own therapist and even attended a few group therapy sessions with a child therapist with the kids. At first, Jim visited every other weekend, but he eventually spent more and more time away.

About a year after the rupture, Deborah got a call from Sarah, a close friend. One of Deborah's teens, Jamie, worked weekends in Sarah's veterinary practice walking dogs. Sarah had called to let Deborah know that another employee had seen Jamie taking money from the practice's register and that she'd personally confirmed the theft from security cameras.

When Sarah confronted Jamie and asked to look in her backpack, she'd not only found the wad of missing cash, but also a baggie of marijuana.

Before Deborah left the house to pick up Jamie, she searched the twins' bedroom, where she found more marijuana as well as vaping oils and paraphernalia. What Deborah would discover over the next several months was a pattern of marijuana use, smoking, and lying.

Although it would be easy enough to dismiss or explain Jamie's behavior as "acting out" in the aftermath of her parents' separation and divorce, we want you to understand that family dynamics are a bit more nuanced than that. Specifically, families work as a system. And in order to understand the person with the identified "problem," it's critical to understand the way the system works within the family.

In another book in this series, *Understanding and Loving a Person with Alcohol or Drug Addiction*, Steve and his co-author Dave Stoop unpacked various roles played in those families. The "dependent" is the person with the core problem. This could be an alcoholic, addict, workaholic, or any other "-holic" in the family. And the other members of the family play the roles of "codependents." Within the family system, the codependents unconsciously protect the dependent from having to face the reality of the problem.

Without ever being aware they're doing it, the codependents in the family take on unique roles within the system. For example, let's consider a family in which one parent is an alcoholic. The "chief enabler," typically played by a spouse, enables the alcoholic by protecting him or her from the consequences of his or her drinking. The enabler might hide the addiction from neighbors, make excuses for absences at social events, or even provide the alcohol. Other family members take on a variety of other roles. The "enabler-in-training," likely one of the children, takes her cues from the chief enabler. The "hero," often the oldest child, makes the family look good with his success. The "scapegoat," who watched an older sibling be "good," ends up acting out some kind of "badness," diverting attention from the alcoholic. The "lost child" stays out of the way, often ignoring her own needs and feelings. The "comic" or "mascot" breaks the tension with his comedy or playfulness, which shifts the attention away from the problem.

Margot was raised in a home fraught with alcoholism, first that of her father and subsequently that of her stepfather. As if following a script, her older brother played the role of the hero, and she easily fell into the role of the lost child. Unwittingly supporting the system, and thus enabling the alcoholic, they dutifully played the roles they didn't realize they were playing.

Do you recognize any of these roles at work in your family of origin or your current family? As long as people play their roles, the system continues to enable the person with the problem.

When outsiders looked at Jim and Deborah's family, often admiring the way the couple continued to work together to care for their children, they would typically identify the "sore thumb" that stuck out, the behavioral "problem," as *Jamie*. And while Jamie's change in behavior likely *was* related to the dissolution of her parents' marriage, there was a bit more going on.

After Jim's disclosure, he experienced great relief. The heavy secret he'd been carrying for years was exposed. Rather than feeling the shame that was rightly his, though, he instead felt a palpable release from the shame he'd been carrying for years. He reported feeling almost euphoric. The shift in his satisfaction wasn't lost on Jim's wife or children. They *noticed* that he was less anxious and was happier.

Because children take their emotional cues from their parents, Jim and Deborah's children unconsciously discerned from their father's behavior that there wasn't room for sadness, for anger, or for fear. To experience any of those "negative" emotions seemed like it would put their relationship with their father at risk, and they didn't want to do that. To preserve the relationship, they smiled and got on board with Jim's decision.

But the feelings were still there. The oldest felt angry. The youngest felt sad. Jamie's twin felt shame. And Jamie felt anger. Rage, really. But because of the way the system worked, there wasn't room or permission for them to notice and experience the feelings they were having. Instead, these codependents protected Jim from the consequences of his actions. Deborah facilitated the FaceTime conversations. Her oldest son stopped attending the campus ministry group he was a part of, suspecting they wouldn't understand. He was avoiding triggering the feelings in himself he wanted to avoid. And guess what? The system worked! Jim was protected.

But keeping feelings bottled up is like trying to hold a beach ball under water. With some effort, it's possible for a while. But eventually, it's going to pop up. And when the family system shifted to protect Jim, the beach ball popped up in Jamie's life. Unwittingly taking on the role of "scapegoat," the family's attention shifted to managing "her problem" rather than honestly confronting and discussing the repercussions the family was experiencing as a result of Jim's disclosure.

It's tricky, right? If you have a child who is using marijuana or some other substance in your family, you may recognize some of these roles. And sometimes individuals will even take on more than one role. (In addition to the "lost child" role Margot played as a girl, she would also play the comic to diffuse tense situations.) Addiction is a family disease, and everybody in the family needs help.

One sibling of a marijuana user might play the "hero" role by getting good grades and joining every club in school. Another child might enable marijuana use by keeping secrets about his or her sibling's friendships and behaviors. Another might even act out in a different way to divert attention from the real problem.

To allow the kind of self-awareness necessary to notice the patterns at work in your family takes courage. When Steve's friend Dave and his wife were participating in a family-focused addiction treatment program in support of one of their children, Dave introduced himself to the group by saying, "I'm here because one of our kids has a problem." A twenty-year-old young man in the group, an alcoholic, challenged Dave: "You're going to find out you're here because *you* have a problem!" To his credit, Dave was willing to see and admit the problem he had that impacted the family system. Dave honestly confessed, "I was the problem because I was preoccupied with my graduate work, even though I thought I had it all in balance within the family." He continued, "But everyone else in the family was subconsciously working hard to protect me from being seen as the 'real problem.'"[1]

Don't miss that. Friends, that is the kind of honest awareness that helps a system finally shift. As we own the roles we've played and refuse to play them any longer, the system can finally change. When we refuse to protect others from the consequences of their choices, change is at last possible.

Are there ways in which you see family members "protecting" your child who uses marijuana? Maybe you or your spouse dole out punishment that doesn't offer any real motivation for your child to change his or her behavior. Perhaps a sibling covers for him or makes excuses about the clear smell of marijuana smoke on her clothes. Or maybe a sibling simply distracts the family with her overachievement or his comedy. Our enabling harms our loved ones by perpetuating the problem.

This isn't about pointing fingers or assigning blame, and we hope Dave's transparency about his preoccupation with his schoolwork demonstrates that. When we're able to notice and own the role we play in our family system, we can finally do something differently.

In *Understanding and Loving a Person with Alcohol or Drug Addiction*, the authors pointed out that our relationships don't always work logically. "You can make a good argument for why the one you love should stop his addictive behavior, and it will make logical sense to everyone except the one you want to change. That's why nagging is useless, and the harder you try to 'get through' to the addict, the more everything stays the same." They challenged family members by saying, "Stop trying to be logical. Stop nagging. Instead, work on yourself and see what happens."[2]

Dave Stoop shared a really helpful story about a couple whose son was addicted. After several years of education and support practicing tough love, this husband and wife took the bold step of reporting to the police that some of the wife's jewelry was missing. When they acknowledged to the officer taking the report that it was possible the thief could have been one of their children, the officer closed the report folder and put his pen in his pocket. It's easy to imagine that his experience with similar families over the years had taught him that most were not willing to pursue legal action against their own. He was surprised when the father assured him, "If it's true, we are committed to pressing charges." As a result of their filing charges, their son spent nine months in jail.

Fellow parents, can you imagine exercising this kind of courage and commitment? But it is a loving act, born of wisdom. Those parents couldn't change their son's behavior, but they could change *their* behavior, and they did. And that courageous choice helped the son to make the decision to turn his life around.

Every family's situation is different, and yours might look a variety of ways today. Maybe your child's behavior is causing you to suspect that he or she might be smoking marijuana. Or it could be that your child is belligerent in admitting and embracing his or her choice to use. Whether your child is fifteen or twenty-five, you cannot control his or her choices. What you can do is control your own. That means two things: You can name and implement consequences for your underage child or your child who is "of age" who is living in your home or receiving any kind of financial support from you. But doing what is in your control also means looking inward to notice and own the role you play in your family system.

Beloved, when you are finally able to see the role you are playing and take responsibility, you are one step closer to transforming the system that is keeping everyone stuck.

Self-Reflection

Margot has a vivid memory of walking down the hall when her daughter was five, peeking into her bedroom, and noticing her sleeping there, safe and secure. Sprawled out on her shiny purple bedspread, she knew her daughter didn't have a care in the world. She lived in a home that was physically and emotionally safe. She knew nothing else.

But Margot's own experience as a five-year-old was very different. Her parents' marriage was crumbling. Her father was drinking and physically abused her mother—and Margot was terrified that she would be next. Decades later, becoming the mother of her own kindergartener brought up a lot of memories and feelings from that age.

Parenting our children can bring up what may be unresolved from our past, both consciously and unconsciously. We want to name the reality that parenting our children can trigger something in us that needs to be resolved. This is an opportunity for us to grow, if we'll only seize it.

For example, let's say that John, now the father of a teen, was raised in an alcoholic home with parents who were demanding, strict, and overly punitive. It's possible that somewhere along the way, John noticed that something inside him needed healing, and he seized opportunities to deal with that hurt. When he went off to college, he may have attended an Adult Children of Alcoholics meeting on campus with a roommate. When a girlfriend called him out on his own drinking, he may have paused to look inside and see how his past was affecting his present. Or maybe as he and his wife prepared to welcome their first child, John may have started to remember what his own childhood home was like and sought the help of a therapist. There may have been all these points on his journey when he had the opportunity to notice the old hurts and seek healing.

But let's say that John did not purpose to resolve his old hurts before parenting his children. Under those circumstances, it would be reasonable to anticipate that John's parenting might look one of two ways.

John might assume, consciously or unconsciously, that all parents are and ought to be demanding, strict, and overly punitive. So he might naturally parent in this way. It's also possible that John might react, consciously or unconsciously, to his parents' authoritarian style by being overly lenient in his own parenting.

When we don't pause to notice what's inside of us—the hurts we endured from well-meaning and ill-meaning parents, caregivers, other adults, and even peers—it has the power to boss us around. We mention this to remind you that parenting your child is an opportunity for you to notice and deal with old hurts that you've not yet faced.

No one will or can force this on you. If you decide to ignore the childhood wounds and traumas you endured, you can knock yourself out denying, avoiding, and repressing them. Alcohol "helps," for a minute, to avoid the pain. Workaholism can numb it, as can countless other addictions. But when you choose to ignore the old hurts, they will continue to interfere with your relationships. You will suffer. And your loved ones will too. We pray that you will seize the opportunity presented to you to pause and work on your own issues. Do it because it is a very concrete way for you to love your child.

CHAPTER 6

Start Making a Difference Today

So many parents Steve encounters are desperate to know that, in a culture that tempts our children toward death-dealing behaviors, they can make a difference in their children's lives. They need to know they can impact their children's lives for good. In *How to Talk to Your Kids about Drugs* (formerly *Drug-Proofing Your Child*), Steve and co-author Jim Burns offer six building blocks to keep kids drug-free that they've seen work over the years.

Because you've chosen to read this book, it's likely that your child is not drug-free. Maybe you noticed the faint smell of marijuana smoke on his clothing and confronted him the very first time he tried it. Or perhaps you are the parent of a young adult living at home who smokes daily and has no interest in stopping. Whether you are the parent of a child who's experimenting with marijuana or entrenched in chronic use, we believe that implementing these six strategies will serve your child.

It's important to us that you hear that it's never too late to implement these foundational strategies.

Give Your Children Time and Attention

If you feel like there's always something more on your "to-do" list that needs to get done, you're not alone. Between the responsibilities associated with one's family, home, job, church, community, and possibly education, a lot of us are *busier* than we'd like to be. Our calendars—the way we choose to use our time—communicate to our children what we value.

When we give our children time and attention, we communicate to them that they're valuable. When we invest time listening to them, we communicate that they're worth seeing and hearing and knowing and loving. When we offer our children our time, we communicate to our children that they're important.

If you're already feeling stretched, this isn't meant to condemn you or make you feel worse. We're hoping, however, to remind you that your schedule is not the boss of you; you are the boss of your schedule. And you have the power to choose to spend time with your children. (If you were looking for an "excuse" to slow down, you've got one.)

If the yard doesn't get raked, the leaves will be there tomorrow.

If the dishes don't get unloaded from the dishwasher, they'll wait patiently until after you've put your babies to bed.

If the head of the deacon board invites you to serve another term, you are not the only person who can fill this role.

If you choose to take a break from social media and other time-stealing phone habits, you won't miss a thing.

Yes, the pace of life can feel overwhelming at times. But you need not play the "victim" of "busyness." The years when your children are at home with you are precious, and we encourage you to be intentional about investing in them.

Give Your Children Integrity

Dorothy Law Nolte wrote a poem titled "Children Learn What They Live" that is instructive here:

> If children learn with criticism, they learn to condemn.

> If children live with hostility, they learn to fight…
> If children live with encouragement, they learn confidence.
> If children learn with tolerance, they learn patience…

As a child living in a home impacted by addiction and violence, Margot grumped internally, "Am I the only one reading this poem?" But today, as a mother of three, it resonates with what she knows now about families: children absorb more than we give them credit for.

While we might think that the "takeaway" we offer our children will be delivered in eloquent lectures or heart-warming dinner prayers or moving admonitions, more often our children are absorbing what they see in us. What they're shown is more compelling than what they're told.

When we tell the truth, even when it's difficult, our children notice.

When we express affection with our spouse, our children notice.

When we share our resources with the church and with those in need, our children notice.

When we practice living with integrity, we give a gift to our children.

Give Your Children Affirmation

The psychologist Abraham Maslow said, "It takes nine affirming comments to make up for each critical comment we give to our children." If we haven't done the therapeutic work of noticing the ways our parents spoke to us when we were growing up, we might not even notice when those critical comments escape our lips. But our children notice, and those words lodge in their deep places.

And because negative words don't really motivate people to change anyway, they are largely wasted words! What really changes children is affirmation and encouragement. Our children need to hear that we believe in them. We encourage you to seek opportunities to offer your children affirmation, praise, and encouragement.

Each of us has a deep longing to be seen, heard, known, and loved. The author of Exodus observed the following:

> But the Israelites continued to groan under their burden of slavery. They cried out to God for help, and their cry rose up to God. God heard their groaning, and he remembered his covenant promise to Abraham, Isaac, and Jacob. He looked down on the people of Israel and knew it was time to act. (Exodus 2:23–25)

Let's look at the posture of a good Father toward His children:

God saw.

God heard.

God knew.

God cared.

We're convinced that every individual is hungry to be seen, heard, known, and loved. And when we purpose to see our children, to listen to them, to notice them, and to respond with care—to affirm them—we bless them.

What is it that makes your child unique in all the world? When do you see him or her really shine? What is it that brings this child joy? How is he or she a blessing to others? What's a character trait that you really admire in your child? Be generous in those things.

Give Your Children Opportunities to Communicate

Sometimes it's hard for parents of sullen and silent teens to remember their children were not only once chatty, but that they craved our time and attention. As long as we gave it to them, they'd babble on about everything and nothing. That's why the season in which many adolescents retreat from us, offering curt one-word answers—“fine,” “yes,” “no,” “okay”—can feel difficult for parents.

Communicating with your children takes work! But it is worth it. Do what it takes to keep the lines of communication open.

One of the ways you do that is by spending time with your children. While this kind of seems like a no-brainer, it’s critically important. The kinds of conversations you hope to have with your children don’t necessarily happen when you think they might. Or when you carefully orchestrate them!

But we do encourage you to carve out time and space to spend with your child, because often this is when the best conversations can unfold. One mother takes a long hike with her son every month. Another plans an annual “Girls Getaway” weekend with her two daughters. One father planned a special week-long camping trip with each of his sons when they turned thirteen. And another dad planned special “date nights” to share with his daughter. These opportunities can enhance the communication process by making space for conversations to unfold naturally. And these intentional opportunities make room for children to feel significant to their parents.

When conversation doesn’t happen naturally, you’ll need to get a little creative. Maybe use a deck of game cards with thoughtful questions already provided and see where the conversation leads. If your child *wants* something from you—permission to go out with friends, an extra hour until curfew, a ride to the mall—that you don't object to, bargain with her for it.

"Sure, sweetie, I'm happy to give you a ride. And on the way, I want you to ask me three questions about when I was your age."

"No problem, son, and when you get home, I look forward to your telling me all about your evening and helping me learn more about your friends."

It takes a bit of thoughtful effort to give your children opportunities to communicate, but it's worth it.

Give Your Children a Network

If you grew up watching *The Waltons* on television, you may remember an intergenerational family, all in one household, that included Grandpa and Grandma. The period in which the show was set depicted the years leading up to World War II in a fictional rural Virginia town. While intergenerational households are less common today, in 1940 about 65 percent of American households had at least one grandparent as a full-time active member. In 1980, though, the number of multigenerational households dipped to a low of only 12 percent,[1] a number that is once again on the rise. Unfortunately, that's not because families are stronger today than they once were. Today more and more grandparents are being tasked with the responsibility of raising grandchildren when their own children (the parents) are unable to do so. Also, families separated by geography aren't raising children with a strong network of grandparents, aunts, uncles, and cousins—eliminating many of the natural supports that were once taken for granted.

It's important for children to have a strong network of support that includes their immediate family and also stretches beyond it, such as a church family that knows and loves them.

One of the boys in the youth group at Margot's church was arrested for a prank that got out of hand. And you know who showed up when he was being held behind bars? The youth pastor who knew him and loved him. Although none of Margot's own kids had trouble with the law during adolescence, the committed youth group volunteers showed up at their soccer, baseball, basketball, and volleyball games. And when her daughter went to the prom, two of the volunteers showed up in advance to do her hair and makeup. That's what a network of loving support looks like.

If your family isn't experiencing this kind of support network right now, you can be instrumental in building one.

Invite college students from your church over for a home-cooked meal and night of board games. Welcome single older adults over to join your family for movie nights. And keep an eye out for international students who might be stuck on campus during the holidays. All of us need a network of loving relationships, and you can be instrumental in building that for your family and for others.

Give Your Children a Spiritual Foundation

Although research shows little difference in drug and alcohol use between Christian and non-Christian young people, one of the most critical factors in avoiding drugs and alcohol is having an active spiritual life. When young people are *actively engaged* with their faith, they are more likely to be drug-free.

Therefore, we encourage you to help your children be involved in the life of the church. When Margot was in high school, the church was the locus of her friendships. She attended Bible Study with girls her age. They sang in the choir and helped produce musicals together. They went to youth group and Sunday school and on ski trips together over spring break. The fact that other teens from church formed her nucleus of friendships was significant in her choices to avoid drugs and alcohol.

If you're the parent of a child who loathes church activities—for any host of reasons, understandable or not—this exhortation may sting for you. You can require a certain amount of participation, but you can't always change your child's attitude. We understand. And we encourage you to be good stewards of your child's spirits outside of congregational life as well. When you have an active spiritual life, your children become witnesses to what a loving relationship with Christ can look like.

And Now, Take Action

These strategies are meant to be lived out, so we want to offer some ideas for action steps you can take this week to begin practicing this kind of intentional parenting.

- **Give your children time and attention.** When there's laundry to be done, groceries to be bought, and bills to be paid, our children can sometimes get our "leftover" time and attention. This week, invite your child to share an activity he or she loves. Silence your phone, leave it at home, and enjoy!

- **Give your children integrity.** This week, examine your heart. As you think about the way you use your financial resources, the way you use your time, the way you use your words, the way you use your "screens," and more, soften your heart and ask God to show you where your life lacks integrity.
- **Give your children affirmation.** Affirmation that sinks deep is more than "You look great today" or "Nice catch in right field." Notice what is unique to your child. Is it his generosity? Her creativity? His care for others? Her thoughtfulness? Then take time this week to name what you see in your children.
- **Give your children opportunities to communicate.** When you're spending that special time with your child this week, keep your antennae up for ways to engage your child in conversation. Take a genuine interest in his friends. Ask some questions about her science fair project. And keep your ears open for the conversation you're not expecting!

- **Give your children a network.** This week, be intentional about pursuing one relationship that will strengthen your child's social network of support. Invite a youth group leader over for ice cream. After dinner, arrange a FaceTime call with grandparents across the country. Or invite a family from church over for dinner.
- **Give your children a spiritual foundation.** This week, engage your child in one spiritual activity at home. Maybe pull out the craft supplies and create the world's most bedazzled prayer list. Or maybe turn on the video camera and record an interview with your child about his or her thoughts on God at this age—one that you can watch together in ten years! Be intentional about engaging your child spiritually.

Whether your child is preschool age and you're thinking forward right now to her adolescence and young adult years, or whether your child has been caught at school with a bag of marijuana, it's never too late to begin investing time and attention to help your child thrive.

CHAPTER 7

Thinking through Family Policy

"Please? Please, please, please?" Ellen begged.

Cassie hadn't heard her daughter whine and beg and plead like that since she was four.

"I really, really, really want to sleep over at Francine's house, and I promise nothing will happen. I promise. Cross my heart," Ellen assured her.

"Let's look at where we are," Cassie said. "In October, you slept over at Francine's, snuck out of her house, met up with a group of guys, and got high."

"And I was grounded forever," Ellen reminded her. "I said I was sorry, and I am."

"Slow down, li'l miss," Cassie answered. "Because when you gave us your word that it wouldn't happen again, we allowed you to sleep over at her house in December over winter break."

Ellen's face fell, recognizing where this was heading.

"Yeah," she interrupted, "but we didn't leave her house. The guys came over, and her parents knew what we were doing, and they thought it was safer to do it in their house than out in the world. It's not like I snuck out or anything. Totally safe."

"We've already discussed 'safe,' and you and I disagree. You know that we expect you to honor the rules we've set for you. You could have texted or called us to ask us for help. But you didn't. You just went along with the crowd."

"But tonight is different," Ellen insisted. "It's totally going to be just girls. Old-fashioned slumber party where we stay up, do Mad Libs, eat popcorn, watch Netflix, and paint our nails."

Cassie doubted the girls would be doing anything involving adjectives and adverbs.

"Sweetie, I don't think you're getting it," she said. "You had our trust. You abused it. And now you've lost the privilege of going to sleepovers since you're unable or unwilling to make good choices."

"But all of my friends are going to be there," Ellen whined.

"I know. It probably feels pretty disappointing," Cassie said sincerely.

She waited for Ellen to turn on her. She knew it was coming. So she wasn't surprised when her daughter bit back.

"You're so mean," Ellen accused. "No one else has parents who try to control their lives."

"I hear that you're angry," Cassie said. "But we're not in this situation because of choices Dad and I made. We're here because you chose to sneak. You chose to use marijuana. You chose to lie. That's not on us."

"This is so unfair," Ellen moaned.

"I know it feels that way. But you make choices that are illegal and unsafe, and it's our job to protect you. We care about you, and we want the best for you."

Forethought

When Ellen was in elementary school, Cassie and her husband had discussed the rules they wanted to enforce in their home about alcohol and drug use. Instead of using the word "rules," though, they named their behavioral expectations "family policy." And they were the makers of policy. They decided what they would expect of their children, why they would expect it, and what the consequences would be if their children chose to behave otherwise.

We acknowledge that parents who are shepherding a child through long division, the all-school spelling bee, girl scout merit badges, and 6:30 a.m. swim team practices deserve their own merit badge for having the foresight to be so intentional about planning ahead for the adolescent years. Most of us are just paddling to stay afloat during those early years.

Whether your children are in diapers and you accidentally picked up this book from the floor of your sister-in-law's minivan, or whether you've been wrangling with your teen over marijuana use for the last eighteen months, we believe that you can always pause, plan, and implement the practices you choose for your home. So we're inviting you to think about "the what," "the why," and "the how."

"The What": The Policy You Will Implement in Your Home

In this process of creating rules, or policies, for your home that protect those you love, the first part—deciding what rules you expect your children to follow—is the most straightforward. Yet we know that many families, including Christian ones, don't do this. They simply don't often pause in advance to anticipate the challenges that may lie ahead for their children, including but not limited to alcohol use, tobacco use, drug use, sexual activity, and more.

If you're married or have a friendly relationship with a former spouse, this is a conversation you need to have, if you haven't already. If you're parenting solo without the support of your children's other parent, we encourage you to seek support from others: friends, pastors, counselors, etc.

For our purposes, we are limiting our scope of "policy-setting" to marijuana use. If you're reading this book, you're likely to expect that all family members will refrain from any use of recreational marijuana.

That simple and reasonable expectation is easy enough to communicate. Ideally, you will have the opportunity to communicate this expectation in any number of conversations you have with your child over the years. But we also know that soccer practices and band camp and youth group and selling baseball candy can threaten to squeeze out some of our aspirations for parenting. If you've found yourself in the position of dealing with your child's marijuana use without ever having forbidden it, know that you're not alone. It happens.

The very best time to communicate that you expect your child to refrain from marijuana was likely a decade ago. But the next best time is *today.* Communicate clearly to your child that those who live in your home are not permitted to use marijuana.

"The Why": The Rationale for the Rules You Will Implement in Your Home

"Is it really that bad?" is what many parents, even Christian parents, are wondering. The fact that marijuana has been legalized in many states has a lot of us wondering how strict we should be. Because medical marijuana *can* offer relief to those enduring physical suffering, many parents today aren't quite sure how to think about it. When many of us were growing up, we "knew" that marijuana was bad because it was illegal. But today, we're no longer sure.

We want to offer some tools to help you think about the boundaries you can establish in your home around marijuana. Two questions can be helpful guides in identifying the rules you want to implement in your home:

- Is it legal?
- Is it harmful?

Is It Legal? Is It Harmful?

Because discouraging our children from participating in anything illegal is pretty much a no-brainer, this is a great place to start.

- Even if marijuana has been legalized in your state, it is always illegal for anyone under twenty-one (with the exception of extremely rare medical uses).
- If recreational marijuana use is illegal in your state, it is illegal for everyone of all ages.

Ideally, you would have this conversation with your children when they're young. In fact, research has shown that talking to your young children about drug and alcohol use and abuse is more effective than you might think. But the reality is that many of us will face the use of illegal substances by our children at the same time they do.

A second question that can help guide your thinking is this: "Is it harmful?" As you consider the rules that will govern your home, and you've already decided that you're unwilling to endorse illegal activities, then if your child is under twenty-one or you live in a state where recreational marijuana use is illegal, your policy on marijuana has been determined for you.

But let's say that you live in a state where recreational use is legal for those over twenty-one. And your son, who enjoys smoking marijuana with his friends, has recently moved home after graduating from college and is arguing that he should be allowed to smoke because it's legal. Yes, you could answer, "My home, my rules." But it will likely be more fruitful for your relationship to be able to offer the *reasons why* that is your household policy.

When Paul was writing to the church in Corinth, he offered guidance on whether believers should eat food that had been sacrificed to idols. The new Christians were arguing that because they were free in Christ, they had the right to do anything. But Paul pushed back: "You say, 'I am allowed to do anything'—but not everything is good for you. You say, 'I am allowed to do anything'—but not everything is beneficial" (1 Corinthians 10:23–24). He went on to exhort the believers to put the good of others before their own interests.

Though adults consuming marijuana recreationally may be "legal" in the state where you live, it might not be either beneficial or constructive. And you have the right to say that in your home, you don't permit that which is harmful.

Is there a scenario in which using marijuana, or parts of the cannabis plant, is beneficial? As we discussed earlier, parents of children suffering from intractable seizures would say "Yes!" The results for these children who are given CBD have been remarkable in reducing the seizures' severity and frequency. But if your child tries to use that as an argument that marijuana is "beneficial," remind him that there is a big difference between recreational marijuana use and medical marijuana use that has been recommended by a physician.

Because our children can get pretty creative in their resistance to the rules we establish, your child might attempt to insist that recreational marijuana is beneficial and not harmful. She might lobby that when she's feeling stressed, marijuana "takes the edge off" and helps her to "cope" or "chill out." As you engage her in conversation, you might push back by reminding her that:

- Recreational marijuana use is not *financially* beneficial. According to the Oxford Treatment Center, the average cost of an ounce of high-quality marijuana is $326.[1]
- Recreational marijuana use is not *spiritually* beneficial. If your child has tried a concentrated strain of marijuana, he might argue that he's had a spiritual experience! And that might be true. But it's fair to argue that if a spirit is not drawing one closer to the person of Jesus, it's not the Holy Spirit sent by the Father that we meet in Scripture.
- Recreational marijuana use is not *relationally* beneficial. While it may make your child feel close to friends who use, being under the influence of

any mind-altering drug makes it more difficult for one to be fully present in the relationships that matter most in life.

- Recreational marijuana use is not *physically* beneficial. Scientists from Amen Clinics examined SPECT scans of 62,454 brains. Chronic marijuana users had decreased blood flow and activity in multiple regions of their brains.[2]
- Recreational marijuana use is not *emotionally* beneficial. While one may perceive that marijuana use reduces his stress or anxiety for a moment, it does nothing to address the source of those feelings.

A Critical Caveat to "Is It Harmful?"

Let's say that marijuana is legal in your state for those over twenty-one, and you've reasoned with your adult child living at home that you forbid the use of mind-altering drugs because they're not beneficial or constructive out of love for him or her: "I don't want to support something that will hurt you or others."

That's solid logic. But it will not convince the astute child—of any age—who sees you making choices that are not beneficial to yourself or others. What kind of example have you set?

- Has your drinking ever interfered with your relationships?
- Has your compulsive shopping driven your family into deep debt?
- Has your use of pills ever made you unavailable to your child?
- Has your chronic overeating compromised your physical health and safety?

If you're asking your child to refrain from activities that harm himself or others, it's important to apply the same standard to yourself.

And if you *do* recognize an inconsistency in this area, this may be the moment to make the change that will benefit yourself and your family.

Setting policies keeps your family safe and healthy. You serve your children when you can clearly articulate the rules for your home and why you've chosen them.

CHAPTER 8

Three Guiding Principles for Parents

In ways we likely can't fathom or measure, the home in which we were raised informs the way we parent our children. Even when we vow to do things differently, simply doing the exact opposite of what our parents did won't necessarily be the best way to parent our children. That's why books like this and resources like New Life Ministries are critical in helping us begin to do things differently. Most of them will seem like plain common sense. But for those of us who might not have been dealt a lot of common sense or seen it modeled, it's helpful to hear these statements articulated clearly:

1. "We're not going to support your doing anything that's illegal or harmful."
2. "Our house, our rules."
3. "It's not our problem. It's your problem."

"We're Not Going to Support Your Doing Anything That's Illegal or Harmful."

"Brad's parents are going to be home," Andrew said. "They're totally fine with it. No one's going to drive. It's totally safe."

"We hear you," Andrew's mother confirmed, "but we aren't allowing you to sleep over at Brad's and smoke marijuana because we can't support your doing anything that's illegal or harmful."

"But it's legal in our state!" Andrew argued.

"Not for anyone under twenty-one," Andrew's father reminded him.

"And no one's going to drive, so it's not dangerous..." Andrew continued to protest.

"We're not going to get in the weeds over this one," his dad answered, "but it actually is damaging. It harms the brain and puts users at risk for other complications as well."

"But..."

"Andrew," his mother calmly stated, "we know you're disappointed, but your safety isn't negotiable. We're not allowing you to go to the sleepover."

The policy in Andrew's home was that the parents wouldn't permit anything illegal or harmful, and allowing

Andrew to attend a sleepover where marijuana was being used clearly fell under that umbrella.

But other situations aren't quite so cut and dried. Even if you're the kind of parent who would never host a beer party for teens or give your kid money for weed, you might be inadvertently supporting your child's marijuana use in other subtle ways.

Maybe you give your child an allowance or spending money to use at her discretion. If she's using that money on alcohol or drugs, you're supporting her doing something illegal. But it might be even more nuanced than that.

For instance, if you're paying for your college-aged child to live in a dorm or rent an apartment with friends, and he's using the money he makes from his part-time job to buy weed, part of what makes that possible is that you're paying his living expenses.

Steve suggests framing it this way: "Nowhere in our country is marijuana legal for anyone under twenty-one. You're acting like you're an adult. Adults pay for their own gas, rent, food, and insurance. We're not going to pay for those things so that you have money to spend on illegal things."

That can be mind-boggling for some parents. All your child's life, you've dutifully met his every need—food, shelter, clothing, education—without batting an eye. You shelled out dollars without giving it a second thought. Yet as your child grows in independence, it may be time to give a second thought to the ways that you are supporting him.

"Our House, Our Rules."

"Mom, all of my friends are vaping. It's just not that big of a deal."

"Carson's mom doesn't have a problem with it."

"Dad, I'm going to be able to do it when I go to college in six months anyway, so why not now?"

If your child is fervent about wanting to consume marijuana, he will offer a barrage of arguments about why he should be allowed to do it. But there's likely one reality that your child has overlooked.

When you are the adult paying for the mortgage and utilities, you get to make the rules. You decide what is permissible in your home and what is not. When their children were young, Steve's wife determined that as the heads of the household, they had a Bill of Rights: "We pay the bills; we have all the rights."

There might be any number of reasons you decide that marijuana use isn't permissible for anyone living in your home.

Maybe you're opposed because it's illegal or because of the harm marijuana does to the developing brain. Though you don't *owe* your child an explanation for the rules you establish for your home, sharing your logic might help him understand why you've made the decisions you have.

This might feel much more authoritarian than you prefer. And your child will likely agree! But "my house, my rules" is actually the most *loving* way to care for your child. If insisting on being the rule-maker feels more domineering to you than you'd prefer it to be, take some time to consider why that might be the case. And if you can agree that keeping your children from harm by establishing house policies is the loving way, we pray you will gather your courage and make it happen.

"It's Not Our Problem. It's Your Problem."

Kara dashed in late to work, throwing her coat on a hook and dropping into her chair.

"Sorry I'm late," she said to her officemate, Jane. "You know we've been dealing with Mike's marijuana problem. We took his car privileges away, and he woke up late, so I had to drive him to school."

"That's rough," Jane said.

"I actually have to work some overtime today. Since he lost his job after stealing from his boss—to buy weed!—he can't afford to pay for all the soccer gear the team requires."

"Wait, what?" Jane asked.

"We have to find extra money to pay for soccer stuff, so I'll be working late."

"Girl!" Jane challenged her friend. "Mike doesn't have a problem with marijuana; *you* have a problem with marijuana!"

She wasn't wrong. Too often, good and well-meaning parents end up making their child's problem *their* problem. If your child has a problem with pot, then let the child have a problem with pot. You actually *want* the child to have a problem with pot—not you.

When the usual consequences haven't worked—taking your child's phone, cutting off the internet, grounding, etc.—the child doesn't have a problem with pot; *you* have a problem with pot.

If you continue to lend your child your car and he uses it to go buy weed, your child doesn't have a problem with weed; you have a problem with weed.

If you're giving your child a weekly allowance that he's using to purchase marijuana, your child doesn't have a problem with marijuana; you have a problem with marijuana.

Keep the problem where it should be—*with the child.*

Their problem becomes your problem when you don't follow through on the consequences you've established or when you introduce consequences that will help your child change his or her behavior.

These three principles—not supporting what's illegal or harmful, establishing and enforcing clear house rules, and letting the child own his problem—will help you help your child. And once you've implemented the policy, it's time to enforce it.

CHAPTER 9

Implementing Family Policy

One couple, who we'll call Jan and Pete, discovered marijuana in their son's bedroom a few weeks after he had graduated from college and moved back home. After discussing their concerns and making their expectations clear, Jan and Pete let Paul know he was welcome to continue living in their home as long as he agreed to refrain from using marijuana. The plan they outlined was clear: If signs suggested Paul was using marijuana or spending time with those who did, he would have six weeks to make other living arrangements. Specifically, he would need to secure a job and an apartment. At the end of those six weeks, he was no longer welcome to live in their home.

When Paul came home one Saturday night reeking of smoke, he tried to skirt past his parents, who were reading in the living room. When they invited him in to chat, they both smelled marijuana.

"Son, we made our expectations clear, and you disregarded them," Pete said. "Today is May 18, so by July 1, you'll need to be living someplace else."

Paul's eyes widened in disbelief.

"But Dad—" he protested.

Calmly, without anger or anxiety, Pete simply restated the consequence. "Because of your choice, you'll not be living here after June 30."

Hearing the conviction in his father's voice, Paul left the room in a huff.

Turning toward his wife, Pete saw his wife's face racked with pain.

"Honey," she began, "I know we said this would happen, but I really don't think he can do it. I don't think he can get a job or an apartment on his own."

Her voice cracked as she fought back tears.

"We're here if he needs help with an application or reference. But this is his choice, and he's going to live with the consequences."

Though grieved, Jan knew her husband was right.

Her concerns were justified. When six weeks had passed, Paul hadn't done the work to find an apartment and only had a part-time job as a waiter. When his parents remained committed to the plan they'd outlined, Paul angrily packed a few bags and left the house. He texted a friend who picked him up and let him stay at his family's home. When that became untenable, Paul continued to couch surf between his friends' homes.

Four months later, Paul begged his parents to let him come back and live at home, swearing that he wouldn't use marijuana. He'd gotten a full-time job at an upscale restaurant and was saving money to get an apartment with a friend. Sensing his sincerity, Pete and Jan told Paul that if he'd like to come home, there would be certain expectations—including not using marijuana—and they'd all sign a contract agreeing to them.

That did the trick. Paul moved back in—and when he left his parents' home five months later to move into an apartment, it was his own choice.

Boundaries

Some parents are reluctant to establish and enforce clear limits that include consequences for certain behaviors. Others knew how to set those boundaries when their children were three and four but now aren't quite as confident about establishing limits as their children age. If you're in that second camp, know that it is totally appropriate to establish limits, boundaries, rules, and expectations for your underage children and for those who might be of age but are living in your home.

Implementing a Plan

Part of the stigma of "kicking your child to the curb"—real or imagined—is the assumption that an unwitting child is the hapless victim of a parent's sudden whim. And we'd likely agree that if a family has never discussed drug use and a young person comes home smelling like marijuana smoke, it's likely not the best course of action to immediately eject him or her from the home.

The responsibility of discussing the use of drugs, its dangers, and the clear consequences lies with the parent. Ideally, those family conversations happen *before* a child experiments with drugs, but they can happen at any point in the parenting process. When we suggest that parents establish clear consequences for the teen or the young adult who is living at home, we don't mean that those consequences are arbitrary or sudden.

Parents can feel stuck if they believe their only options are allowing their child to smoke pot or "kicking them out of the home." We've seen the most success in families that have chosen to implement a plan.

- **A good plan details clearly the nature of what is considered an offense.** For example, "You're not to smoke in our home, and you're not to smoke outside of the home while you're living here." Or "We're not going to split hairs about whether you smoked or vaped. We're asking you to not use marijuana." Or "We're also asking you not to spend time with friends who are smoking. So if you come home and your clothes smell like weed, the consequences we've outlined will go into effect."
- **A good plan makes consequences clear.** "If you choose to use marijuana again, you can no longer live here. You will be responsible for finding a new place to live and also finding a way to pay for that."
- **A good plan establishes a clear timeline for implementation.** "If signs indicate that you have chosen to use marijuana, you will have six weeks to find another place to live."

Establish a clear plan that you are committed to executing when a child violates family policy.

Rewards and Consequences

The consistent message we want to communicate to families is that it's best to begin talking about drug use with your children early. But we also recognize that families are managing a lot! We have a vision of all we want to instill in our children as they grow, but in the meantime, we're also trying to keep up with the dishes, laundry, and lost ballet shoes. If you're still on the front end of this journey or if you're in a position to coach or shepherd someone who is, we encourage you to start early.

When Steve's daughter, Madeline, was younger, he told her, "If you decide to make good choices throughout high school, there are cash prizes available. I'm going to help you with college and get you a car."

Specifically, he was asking her to refrain from having sex and using drugs or alcohol.

In addition to the desirable long-term rewards, there were also some more immediate consequences if she chose to do the things he'd named as being off-limits. If she broke those rules before she got her driver's license, she would lose the privilege of getting one.

If she broke them after she got her license, she would not have the privilege of using a family car.

Madeline graduated from high school having never touched a drop of alcohol or smoked a joint. Steve also jokingly contends that she's the only virgin ever to have graduated from Laguna Beach High School.

The rules were clear, but so was the fact that Madeline made those choices. Steve says he could have implemented the same system for another child and gotten the opposite results.

What if it hadn't worked? If the consequences Steve had set out didn't alter his child's behavior, he would have said: "There's a boarding school in Ireland, and I'll send you there. And we'll see if *their* consequences alter your behavior."

Forget Ireland—this principle of consistently implementing consequences happens right where you live. Does your child come home smelling like pot? Then he has lost the privilege of going out with his friends. Does your child sneak out of the house to be with his friends? Then he has lost other privileges.

Ideally, naming and consistently implementing consequences for your child's choices will take the burden—the worry and the fury—off of you and place it squarely where it belongs: on your child. Calmly and consistently enforcing the consequences you've established for particular behaviors means that you no longer have to rage—which really wasn't working anyway.

What about Consequences for the Most Challenging Behaviors?

Steve and his wife have a blended family; she brought two boys into the marriage, and Steve had Madeline. One of their sons began making poor choices as a teen, and by the time he was sixteen, he had really gone off the rails. At that time, they sent him to a specialized program in the Utah wilderness—during winter. Steve applauds his wife for being willing to allow this bold and courageous move. That was a difficult season for them all, but when their son returned home, he was a different young man who was proud of what he'd accomplished. Over time, they watched him become an incredible man because they did what they needed to do at the right time.

Do what you need to do when you need to do it.

That philosophy isn't just for sixteen-year-olds making life-threatening decisions. It can be implemented when a toddler reaches for the stove. Or when a middle schooler steals money from her teacher's desk. Or when a college student buys alcohol for his younger brother. Do what you need to do when you need to do it.

What about Consequences for Unanticipated Behaviors?

When Margot's children were younger, she wasn't quite as forward-thinking as Steve was with his children in terms of naming the rewards and consequences for avoiding or embracing unwanted behaviors. And what parent could have imagined twenty years ago that a child with a telephone who was grounded at home could still have unlimited video access to his or her significant other!

It is impossible to anticipate every possibility. So if you're caught off-guard by behaviors you've not anticipated, don't be too hard on yourself. Just because you didn't anticipate it doesn't mean you can't enforce reasonable consequences.

Don't Keep Using Consequences That Don't Work

Chandler and Sarah are the parents of two teens: sixteen-year-old Chris and twelve-year-old Cheryl. Chris attended a fairly liberal private school where, during his ninth-grade year, he'd befriended some guys who used marijuana regularly. During Chris's sophomore year, Chandler and Sarah consistently enforced consequences when Chris broke the house rules—grounding, no phone, no video games—but none of the consequences, which were doled out for longer periods each time, changed Chris's behavior.

During the spring of Chris's sophomore year, Chandler and Sarah had a heart-to-heart talk with their son, letting him know that because of his choices, he wouldn't be returning to the school he'd been attending.

That summer, Chris was enrolled at the local public school in his community. It had all the challenges and temptations of any high school, but his parents had made the decision to switch schools to give Chris the opportunity to take a break from the friends with whom he'd gotten caught up. Moving from a smaller student body to a larger public high school meant that Chris was a little fish in a large pond.

Socially, Chandler and Sarah restricted Chris from spending time with his old friends. And when he started at the new school, Chris was able to reconnect with some other friends he'd known from middle school and sports leagues.

When the consequences we've laid down and enforced don't motivate a child to change his or her behavior, it's time to try something new.

Don't be afraid to go bigger.

One Useful Tool: Blame Us!

One of the important roles we can play as parent is offering our children useful tools to help them navigate life's tricky situations. We understand that if our children end up with a group of kids who are making bad choices, it can be hard for them to resist alcohol, drugs, or other dangerous behaviors.

When Margot's kids were in high school, she and their dad encouraged them to "blame" them when offered alcohol or drugs. They were happy to be the "bad guys" when the children found themselves in uncomfortable situations.

"Sorry, guys, I can't smoke pot because my parents are drug-testing me regularly."

Coaches are also likely happy to take the fall: "We promised Coach we'd stay clean after the season ended."

And if their children got into a difficult or dangerous bind while out with friends, they made it clear they would not be penalized if they called them up to ask for a way out or a ride home.

Once you've established your family policy, implement it consistently.

CHAPTER 10

When Parents Aren't on the Same Page

Hank and Virginia have been married twenty-five years and are the parents of two teen boys. Hank, who attends church occasionally and somewhat reluctantly with his family, is an alcoholic. He functions well enough at his job as an attorney, but his drinking often leads to raging and shameful behaviors at home. Virginia, a staunch Southern Baptist, rarely calls him out on his drinking or his ugly behavior. She's discussed it with her sons, who want her to stand up for herself and for them, but for a variety of reasons, she's not willing to rock the boat.

When seventeen-year-old Joshua was suspended from school for having pot in his locker, Hank and Virginia were called into the vice principal's office to discuss the stipulations for his returning to school. Because Hank didn't think that Joshua's infraction was a big deal, he refused to attend the meeting. Virginia, who was very upset by Joshua's choices, met with the vice principal alone.

That evening when Hank got home from work, Virginia wanted to discuss Joshua's consequences. She invited Hank into the bedroom and closed the door.

"What's the big deal?" Hank asked. "It's just a little pot. That's not going to hurt him. He's a kid. He's trying things. He's figuring it out."

"But it's a gateway drug, and who knows what will be next?" Virginia protested. "Maybe cocaine. Maybe that crystal meth. We just don't know."

The two went back and forth until Hank got fed up and stomped out of the room. Virginia had already told their son that they'd be discussing what the consequences would be after dinner, but that conversation suddenly felt impossible.

If you and your partner are not on the same page when it comes to how you deal with the issue of a child's marijuana use, you're not alone. When it comes to raising children, many couples have differing opinions on how to do it. Sometimes that difference arises from their families of origin. Other times, spouses might have different religious experiences that inform their parenting. And sometimes, as in the case of Hank and Virginia, a parent's own poor behavior can make it difficult to see clearly.

Steve suggests that there's only one path forward for these couples, and that is seeking out the help of a marriage counselor. When couples experience a sizable difference in viewpoints, it can be incredibly helpful to have the input of a third party. It's what Steve and his family have practiced, and time and time again, they've seen it work. He and his wife each see a counselor individually every week. And every other week, they go to a marriage counselor together. Basically, they practice what Steve preaches.

Part of the solution to helping your child is for you to get support in a counseling session. When you find yourself overwhelmed or stuck at home, some of the pressure is relieved because you can say, "We don't have to figure this out right now because we're going to talk with the counselor on Thursday." Parents choosing to get help will help their children.

When Your Spouse Won't Do the Work to Get on the Same Page

Not every parent has a spouse who's available and willing to engage in counseling for the sake of their family.

Some are parenting solo because they've never had a partner.

Some are parenting alone because the child's other parent is uninterested, uninvolved, or unavailable (or just downright difficult).

A married parent might bear the weight of the parenting decisions because his or her spouse has abdicated his or her responsibility.

And other married parents have a partner whose philosophy, attitudes, and practices vary greatly from theirs.

In each of these situations, a parent does not have a loving, supportive partner with whom to co-parent.

If you find yourself parenting without a supportive partner, we want you to know there are resources you can access to find the support you need. You can seek help from a counselor. There are codependency groups that can help you. And there are other support groups for parents that can be beneficial to you.

How to Find a Counselor

If you've been to counseling, you either know what a blessing it is to land with a therapist who's a good fit or you know how fruitless it can be to meet with a therapist who isn't! (Or possibly *both*.) Some parents feel overwhelmed by the task of finding the "right" counselor for them or for their child, and it keeps them stuck. If you're looking for the right therapist, either for your child or for yourself, we have two suggestions.

First, we encourage you to dial 1-800-NEW LIFE (639-5433). If the group has therapists in your area, operators know what their specialties are and can send you in the right direction.

Second, Steve suggests calling the biggest church in town that's healthy and asking the pastor's secretary, "Who does Reverend Smith trust? Who does he recommend when someone needs to see a psychologist?" That will likely be a good lead!

If the pastor doesn't make referrals but instead does all the counseling himself, call the next biggest (healthy!) church in town and ask the same question. Then call that counselor.

When you get the counselor on the phone, explain your situation and ask, "Is this something in which you specialize? Or do you refer cases like this? If so, who do you trust?"

Although it will likely require a few calls, finding the therapist you need is worth the effort.

CHAPTER 11

Is There a Problem?

It's natural to want to avoid facing the possibility that our kids are using drugs.

Remember that wee little bundled infant you brought home from the hospital? Or the whirling dervish of toddler energy you met at the adoption agency? At that time, it likely would have felt absurd to imagine your precious little angel smoking pot. Yet as we noted in a previous chapter, by the time they are seniors in high school, 43.7 percent of young people have used marijuana, and 6.4 percent are using it daily. And while many of us are committed to the insistence that it's not "our kids" who are experimenting with drugs, the math suggests that it's actually very possible.

Teens who use marijuana play soccer with our kids. They're in our carpools. They're in our churches. And there's a good chance that they're also in our homes. There is a drastic discrepancy between the number of young people who are using marijuana and the number of parents who think their children are not using it.

Our belligerent insistence that our own babies would never use alcohol or drugs means that a lot of us are not seeing what is happening around us. And if we squeeze our eyes shut to what our children are doing, we risk losing the opportunity to be involved and get our children the help they need.

To parent our children faithfully is not to shut our eyes to any possibility that they might use marijuana. On the contrary, we serve our children best when we entertain the possibility that they could make poor choices. We love them by having the courage to pay attention to what *is*.

Factors That Lead to Drug Use and Abuse

Because you've committed to educating yourself about teen marijuana use and abuse, we want to help by sharing some of the key factors that can contribute to it. Young people sometimes abuse drugs even when their parents seem to have done everything right. Yet mental health professionals agree that some factors can increase the chances that kids will go down that road.

Genetically, some people will be predisposed to chemical dependency. In Steve's experience, teens are much more likely to change when they learn about this biological risk factor than when they are presented with scare tactics. This kind of transparency requires you to be honest about yourself and your family, but your child's well-being is worth it.

Teens are also tempted to try drugs as a result of peer pressure. Hungry for acceptance, they're likely to experiment if their friends are using. When confronted with known marijuana use, one of Margot's children insisted, "I didn't get peer pressured." He believed that "peer pressure" meant his friends were bullying and cajoling him into using it. As parents, however, we understand that the "pressure" can be much more subtle than the obvious verbal pressure.

Another factor contributing to drug use is the parents' attitudes toward alcohol and drugs. Children see, children do. If a parent minimizes substance use and abuse, the child will as well.

Teens can also be tempted to alleviate the stress of a major life event—illness, their parents' divorce, moving to a new community—by using alcohol or drugs. They want to numb the pain.

A fifth factor influencing drug and alcohol abuse is depression. While often complex, with both hereditary and environmental factors at work, Steve points out that an angry or depressed child is prone to drug abuse.

The final factor is one over which you have the most control: your parenting style. Mental health professionals agree that children aren't getting enough supervision. And far too many parents are failing to take their responsibility seriously enough because they're intent on being "buddies" with their children. To be fair, both parents who are too lenient and those who are too strict likely believe their parenting style is the most loving way to raise their children. If you had to guess which side you err on, which would it be?

Is There a Problem with My Child?

Because everyone is better off when a problem is identified early, we want to make sure you have an idea of what signals to notice in your child's behavior. Steve Arterburn and Jim Burns shared these in 1995, and since human behavior hasn't changed since then, they're not outdated![1]

Because some of these are common to adolescence, you need not be alarmed if you recognize a few. Discuss them with your child if you have concerns.

- Secrecy
- Change in friends
- Change in dress and appearance
- Increased isolation
- Change in interests or activities
- Drop in grades
- Getting fired from an after-school job
- Changes in behavior around home
- Staying out all night
- Possession of a bottle of eyedrops (to counter bloodshot eyes)
- Sudden change in diet that includes sweets and junk food (for the "munchies")
- Dropping out of sports

Not-So-Subtle Signals

These signals indicate chemical abuse. If you notice any of these, take action immediately.

- Deep depression accompanied by hours of extra sleep
- Extreme withdrawal from the family
- Increased, unexplained absenteeism from school
- Little or no involvement in church activities
- Increase in mysterious phone calls that produce frantic reactions
- Starting smoking
- Money problems
- Extreme weight loss or gain
- New friends who are older than your child
- Expulsion from school
- Rebellious and argumentative behavior
- Listening to heavy rock or rap music with pro-drug lyrics
- Acting disconnected or "spacey"
- Physically hurting younger siblings
- Attempting to change the subject or skirt the issue when asked about drug or alcohol use
- Changing the word "party" from a noun to a verb
- Discussing times in the future when he or she will be allowed to drink legally

- Spending long periods of time in the bathroom
- Burnt holes in clothes and furniture

Surefire Signs of Chemical Abuse

When you recognize these symptoms, it's likely that your child's problem with alcohol or drugs is not new. Now is the time to intervene.

- Paraphernalia found in the bedroom: strange vials, small bags, mirrors, pipes, tubes, razor blades, cigarette papers, foil, butane lighters, scales, matches, pop cans that have been converted into pipes, bongs, roach clips, eyedrop containers
- Possession of large amounts of money (indicating child could be selling drugs)
- Needle marks on the arms, or clothing that prevents you from seeing your child's arms
- Valuables disappearing from the house
- Arrests due to alcohol- or drug-related incidents
- Frequent bloodshot eyes
- Uncontrollable bursts of laughter for no apparent reason

- A runny or itchy nose that is not attributable to allergies or a cold
- Dilated or pinpoint pupils
- Uncharacteristically puffy or droopy eyelids
- Mention of suicide or an attempt at suicide
- Disappearance or dilution of bottles in the liquor cabinet
- Time spent with people who you know use drugs or alcohol
- Medicine disappearing from the medicine cabinet
- Defending peers' rights to use drugs or alcohol

The first step in getting help for your child and your family is acknowledging that there's a problem.

But Is It a Problem?

When we discover that our children are using marijuana, we often wonder how much of a problem it is. And to be fair, we're getting a lot of mixed messages.

Those who advocate for the legalization of marijuana argue that because it's a natural plant, it must be harmless. At the same time, we recognize the harmful ways marijuana use can interfere with thinking and perception.

We see CBD sold in gas stations in states where marijuana isn't even legal, suggesting that extracts from the cannabis plant aren't harmful at all. But we also have evidence that marijuana smoke damages lungs the way tobacco does.

We are receiving so many conflicting messages that the most responsible and committed parents can feel confused about how problematic marijuana use by teens and young adults is. Yet what we've learned over the last few years is that, although the impact of marijuana use isn't always measurable in the same kinds of ways as other known harmful substances, the complications it brings cause various kinds of difficulties in the lives of those we love.

It harms the developing brain, which is not fully formed until around the age of twenty-five.

It can conflict with our Christian values.

It can injure relationships with parents, friends, and others.

It is illegal everywhere in the United States for those under twenty-one, putting young people at risk of legal consequences.

It is expensive.

It often reduces motivation in users that can lead to problems in school or at work.

For these reasons and others, we believe that recreational marijuana use is problematic and that our loved ones are designed to flourish without it.

We've suggested things to look for that might suggest your child has a problem with marijuana. And we've skimmed a few of the ways marijuana itself can be problematic. But we also want to pose a few more questions about how problematic marijuana might be in your family.

"Is There a Peer Problem?"

In the book *How to Talk to Your Kids about Drugs,* Steve Arterburn and Jim Burns noted that your children's friends make a big difference in the choices they make about drugs and alcohol.

Peers do influence our children, and—if we're honest—our children influence their peers. We acknowledge this. Sociologists report that the greatest influence on teens through the 1960s was their parents. Today, however, teens are heavily influenced by peers. This is true in many areas, certainly when it comes to marijuana use. A study of eight thousand high school students revealed that of those who reported no close friends who used marijuana, less than 2 percent used drugs themselves. Conversely, of the students who reported that "all" their friends used drugs, more than 90 percent admitted to using. While this is in some ways a chicken-and-egg situation—which came first?—we know that the friends with whom our kids spend time matter.

Many parents readily accept that by the time their children are entering adolescence, their window for influencing them has closed. While it is important to appreciate the role peers play in our children's lives, we don't have to forfeit the influence we do have. We encourage you to stay engaged and be proactive in your children's lives at every age.

If you become aware that your child is using marijuana with a particular friend or group of friends, it's important to connect with those kids' parents. You'll learn a lot from those conversations. If the parents minimize or endorse marijuana use, then that's not someone with whom your child should be spending time.

Is There a "Parent" Problem?

Michael and Patricia had four kids spaced out over fifteen years. The youngest was seventeen-year-old Terrence. Michael and Patricia knew that alcohol and marijuana were part of the wrestling team "culture" at Terrence's high school. He'd come home smelling of booze in the past. Because Patricia's niece had been killed by a drunk driver, they were well aware of the dangers of drinking and driving, and they were concerned for their son.

Michael and Patricia reasoned that "boys will be boys." They'd resigned themselves to the fact that Terrence and his friends would be drinking and smoking *someplace*, so they chose to host a party at their house. They would purchase the alcohol but not the drugs. (The implication was that they wouldn't condemn drugs; they just wouldn't provide them.) All the boys on the team would sleep over so that no one was driving under the influence. If it was under their roof, they reasoned, they could make sure the kids stayed safe.

If this logic troubles you, know that it troubles us too. Not only were Terrence's parents doing something illegal, but they also seemed unaware of the messages they were sending children about substance use and abuse.

If there's a spectrum of parental awareness and acceptance of teens' use of alcohol and drugs, Michael and Patricia land on the far end. However, there are lots of parents in the middle who are unwilling to confront the obvious signs that their children are in trouble and need help. And while they might not be complicit in the ways Terrence's parents were, they deny, compensate, and even enable their children's ongoing substance abuse.

Here are a few red flags that parents are *hurting* their children instead of helping them.[2] Take your time with this list. Don't rush through it. After each behavior, with loving honesty, notice whether it's one in which you've participated.

- Trying to cover up children's irresponsible behavior rather than discussing it openly with a spouse, school counselor, or friend
- Feeling that no matter how hard you try, you can do nothing to change your child's behavior
- Spending an inordinate amount of time talking to your children about problems and pleading for change
- Always questioning what you do and say, thinking that if you change, your kids might be motivated to change
- Giving money to your kids behind your spouse's back
- Spending a large part of your day worrying about the kids and their problems
- Regularly sacrificing for your children, always putting their needs before your own

- Feeling a growing need to control your kids' behavior (rather than release them to greater independence)

If you recognize any of these behaviors in yourself, find someone you trust and share your heart with them.

Doctor, Heal Thyself

The ways that Michael and Patricia enabled their child to behave illegally are plain. Explicit. Intentional. But there are more subtle ways we might be influencing our children to embrace substance abuse of which we're less aware.

When the first thing Dad does after work is pour himself a drink, and there aren't evenings when he doesn't drink, a child learns to alter the way he feels with substances.

Even if Mom thinks her children don't notice that she's overmedicating with prescription pills, a child learns that she doesn't have to tolerate negative feelings; instead, she can erase them by using substances.

These are parents who don't want their children to use marijuana. Yet what they're communicating with their actions—which is more powerful than what they say with their words—is that it's acceptable to alter our moods, avoid our negative feelings, or make ourselves feel better by turning to substances. They'd never dream of articulating those messages explicitly, but it's exactly what they're communicating with their choices.

Whether our addiction of choice is gambling, pornography, or retrieving and tearing open the box from Amazon Prime four times a week, we'd like to convince ourselves that our children don't notice. But they do. And our actions are speaking louder than our words. Not only does our behavior subtly endorse our children's misuse of substances, but it also compromises our authority as parents. Even if your child never challenges your behavior outright, her respect for your authority, wisdom, and counsel has likely been compromised.

If you've discovered that your child is using marijuana, by all means take the steps to help him or her. But as you do, we implore you to notice and take responsibility for the ways that your own behaviors might quietly be endorsing the poor choices your child is making.

Maybe you're the spouse or the former spouse of the parent who is nursing an addiction. We recognize that you're in a particularly tricky spot and have likely asked your child's other parent to change—but without results. We understand the bind you're in. And while we acknowledge that you likely have little control over that person's choices, you can begin to make new choices yourself that will bless your child. Specifically, we encourage you to begin attending Al-Anon or other similar meetings for family members of alcoholics and addicts. While it takes courage to walk in the door the first time and find your seat among a group of strangers, they likely won't be strangers for long. And we promise you that getting this kind of support for yourself will equip you to understand and love both your spouse and your child better.

Here are a few questions to noodle on as you weigh the problems your child and your family may be facing:

- Are there friendships in my child's life that put him or her at greater risk for marijuana use?
- Are there signs that my child is using marijuana or other illicit substances?
- Could I, as a parent, be contributing to the problem in a deliberate way by sponsoring my child's behavior?
- Could I, as a parent, be contributing to the problem in a less intentional way with my own personal behavior?

We know it takes courage to notice and own a problem within your family. We're praying for the holy boldness you need to recognize a problem in your child or in yourself. You can do this.

CHAPTER 12

Learning to Talk to Your Child about Marijuana

"Timmy, sit down!" his father shouted as he walked in the door.

"Actually," Timmy said, "I'm just grabbing my wallet. Luke and I are going to the mall."

"Well," his dad barked, "your mother found a bag of weed in the pocket of your jeans today!" The barrage continued. "I'm not surprised, given the lowlifes you hang around with. Like that no-good Luke in my driveway right now. You're both idiots. Always asking for money to get this or that. To go to a movie. To go out to eat."

"Dad, you don't even—" Timmy protested.

"Shut up," his dad interrupted. "You're just throwing your life away."

A horn honked in the driveway.

"Dad, I gotta go," Timmy said as he breezed past his father and out the door.

"This isn't over!" his father yelled before slamming the door behind his son.

Consider a similar scene in another home.

"Hey, Jimmy," his father said as he walked in the door. "I'd love to talk to you right now."

"Landon's in the driveway, and we're going to the mall."

"You can let Landon know to go on without you, or I can."

"Uhhh..." Jimmy hedged. "Okay, I guess. I'll be right back."

After dismissing his friend, Jimmy joined his dad in the living room.

"Son, when your mom did laundry today before she went to work, she found a bag of marijuana in your pocket."

Taken off guard, Jimmy was silent.

"Can you tell me more about that?" his dad asked.

After some hemming and hawing, Jimmy eventually confessed to having smoked marijuana a handful of times with Landon and two other friends.

Without a tone of anger, fear, or shame, Jimmy's father calmly asked his son to share more about the choices he'd been making.

"I agree that it's hard to refuse when your friends are smoking and inviting you to join. That makes sense," he said.

After more time listening, he told Jimmy how they'd proceed.

"Your mom and I have let you know that we don't permit marijuana use in this home or by people who live here. What you're doing is illegal, and there's a reason for that—because it's harmful. And it's damaging your brain, which is still developing."

His father reiterated the consequences upon which the family had already agreed. Jimmy was reminded that he wouldn't be spending more time with Landon or his other friends and that he was grounded and had lost his phone privileges. But before receiving Jimmy's phone and sending him to his room, his dad gave him a hug.

"Son," he said, "your mom and I think you're a very special young man, and we believe that you were made for so much more than this. We'd like to see you make some changes, and we're here to help you do that."

Silent, Jimmy sulked off.

It's important to be intentional about planning the kind of conversation you want to have with your child about marijuana.

What Have You Experienced?

How did your parents talk with you about marijuana?

A lot of families are silent about marijuana until they no longer have the luxury of not speaking about it. And then a lot of families get suddenly loud. When we talk with our kids about tricky topics like drug use, it can be tempting to announce the house rules and enforce the consequences. No discussion. End of story.

But we want to challenge you to be a little more nuanced than that. Specifically, we want to encourage you to prioritize relationships over rules. Are there rules and expectations in your house that all are expected to follow? Absolutely. Will there be consequences when those rules are broken? You bet. But that's not where conversations need to begin. They begin with listening to your child and seeking to understand and love him or her. Eventually, you'll get to the consequences. And we promise, it's likely no one will be feeling very chatty after that.

Have you noticed that the more anxious and alarmed parents get about risks, the easier it is for an adolescent or young adult to dismiss them? While the risks of marijuana are real, avoid telegraphing your anxiety to your child. It's more prudent for you to keep your cool. Create a space for conversation where your child feels seen, heard, known, and loved.

Prioritize Your Relationship with Your Child

Let's start by looking at the big picture. In a world saturated with stimuli and distractions—as you and your child are both constantly receiving texts, social media alerts, and reports of Amazon deliveries—it is too easy to live parallel lives, even under the same roof, without really engaging with your teen and young adult children. Steve has seen way too many parents who are willing to abdicate a relationship with their child by reasoning, "Oh, well, he's a teen. He's not interested in relating to me anymore" or "I miss the days when she adored me, because now we don't have a relationship since she's only interested in her friends."

Yes, relating to your child looks different now than it did when she was a toddler. But there's no reason you have to give up on having a relationship with your child during her teen and young adult years. Will you have to put effort in? Yes. Will you need to exercise creativity? You will. But there's no reason that you can't find ways to engage the most reluctant young person.

Let's say your child wants to tell you about three YouTube videos that sound like the dumbest things you've ever heard of. Steve encourages you to express interest and also invite a quid pro quo. For instance, "I want to hear all about what interests you, but you need to ask me three questions about sex before marriage."

It just got interesting, didn't it?

"I want you to tell me about the outer nether regions of the land in your video game, and I also want you to ask me three questions about how to succeed."

"Why don't we watch an episode of your favorite show together and then let me ask you three questions about the characters?"

Now you're relating rather than living parallel lives while you coexist under the same roof.

Prepare Yourself for Conversations with Your Child

We encourage you to educate yourself about marijuana use and abuse in advance of the conversations you'll have in your family. Reading this book is a good start!

One of the reasons we think this is so important is because communicating an idea is most compelling when it can be backed up with evidence. In addition to the information we're sharing here, you can find the most up-to-date facts about teen drug use and abuse by visiting a few reliable sources online, such as:[1]

- The U.S. Centers for Disease Control and Prevention

- The National Institute on Drug Abuse
- The American Psychological Association
- The National Institutes of Health

While you don't want to barrage your child with statistics and data, you do want to equip him or her with accurate information about the effects and risks of marijuana use.

Communicate What Matters Most to You

Remember in the story of "Goldilocks and the Three Bears" how one bowl of porridge was too hot? And one was too cold? But one of those three bowls of porridge was *just right*? The same applies to the ways you can communicate with your children.

For example, if you simply tell your kids "Marijuana is bad," you've said too little. Your communication isn't compelling. But if you can offer your children some evidence for your conviction that using marijuana isn't the best choice for them to make, they're more likely to agree.

Likewise, if you ramble on and on about the history of cannabis use over the last six centuries and unpack cannabis-related legislation in the United States over the last one hundred years, squeezing in a horror story about the son of a college friend who became psychotic after using marijuana, you've likely said too much. Before you talk to your child about marijuana, decide what is most important for you to communicate.

Maybe you decide that what's most important is the fact that…

- No state has legalized marijuana use for those under twenty-one because it's harmful to the developing brain
- The immediate effects of using it include legal consequences and impairment that affects your safety, academic performance, coordination, and relationships
- The long-term effects include brain aging, lung damage, and a higher risk of developing mental illness or addiction
- God made you to experience what Jesus calls "life that really is life," and using marijuana can compromise the good plan God has for you

If you have a plan for what's most important for your child to hear, you'll be more likely to communicate effectively.

Make Room for the Truth

As we think about setting the stage to have a fruitful conversation with our kids, all of our best-laid plans and practices will be challenged if our children choose to lie. When our children know they've done something wrong, especially when they know there will be consequences, they can get a little desperate. Some are desperate to stay out of trouble, and if they think that lying will save them from consequences, they're willing to do it.

While your children are responsible for choosing the truth, we encourage you to set the stage in a way that facilitates honest conversations.

We inspire our children to tell the truth when we demonstrate that we can handle the truth. If we've reacted to tough news before with overwhelming anger, sadness, or larger-than-life fear, they may be tempted to lie to avoid our intense feelings.

Guess what this requires of you? It requires you to be *grown*. It means that when your child is honest and shares something that you don't want to hear, you are able to manage your emotions in a mature way. Sure, you may feel sad or mad or afraid, and there's a moment for you to feel those emotions and notice what they're telling you. But what's most important in the moment is that your child trusts you enough to share something difficult, and your job is to be trustworthy. Be present. Be grown. When you handle yourself with emotional maturity, you create an environment where your child knows that he or she can tell you the truth.

You might also consider letting your child know that because you value honesty, if he or she practices it—rather than hiding, lying, or sneaking—your response will be better than if you find out the truth another way.

- "If you've been drinking at a party, you can call me to come pick you up."
- "I don't want you sleeping with your boyfriend, but if you are, we need to be talking about it."
- "Our rule is no marijuana, but if you make a mistake, you can tell us about it."
- "There will still be consequences, but things will go better for you if you come to us with the truth than if we have to get a call from the vice principal, your friend's dad, or a youth pastor. When you create a safe space for your child to tell the truth, he or she is more likely to do it."

Invite Your Child to Offer Solutions

Throughout the remainder of this book, we'll be encouraging you get curious. Put your detective cap on and purpose to know your child more deeply. Ask good questions and then listen well to the answers.

Part of this listening process is being attentive to what's going on inside your child that might cause him or her to use marijuana. Learn more about your child's friends. Pay attention to her feelings. Be aware of changes, losses, or ruptures she may have endured. Listen with the aim of understanding what's going on inside your child.

Another part of the listening process is to invite your child to offer his or her own solutions to the problem at hand. As you know, solutions that sprout from the ground up are typically more effective than those delivered from the top down. Although you may think that you have all the answers, you might be surprised at what your child offers if you ask him to identify some strategies or solutions that will help him change his behavior.

One child of parents who listened well suggested that he could spend less time with a friend who was likely to be present when he got into trouble. As you might imagine, had the parents offered the exact same solution, it would not have been nearly as well-received!

One child suggested that he could use his medical condition as a reasonable excuse to avoid marijuana when his friends offered it. Having the answer as a fallback empowered him to say "no" because he felt that his refusal was now justifiable.

Another child decided that she wanted to break up with the boyfriend who had been encouraging her to smoke weed. When her parents listened attentively to what their daughter shared without judging her or her boyfriend, they made room for her to make her own decision about the young man.

We think you might be surprised when you invite your children to offer solutions to the problems in which they find themselves mired. When you make room for your children to participate in this way and practice listening well, you make room for them to discover their own solutions.

Trust Your Gut

"I knew Blake was using marijuana right away because I have such a strong sense of smell. His clothes stank."

Blake's mother, Susan, shared her family's story. Blake was sixteen, attending a privileged private school, and had been spending time with a new group of friends.

"I knew," she continued, "before he knew that I knew."

Before Susan and her husband leveled any accusations at their son, they began to pay attention, looking for evidence. They noticed who he was spending time with. They utilized the Life360 app to see where Blake was going with friends after school. They paid attention to his body and behaviors. They checked his room. After about a week, they felt certain their son was using marijuana. But when the three of them sat down together, Blake denied ever using it, claiming that the smell on his clothes was from being with other kids he didn't know. (He was clever enough not to throw his own friends under the bus!)

"No," Susan calmly insisted, "I absolutely know. You can't lie."

As Blake continued to deny, lie, and blame, Susan and Greg stood firm.

Finally, when he realized that his lies couldn't help him, Blake confessed to smoking marijuana with his new friends.

While it's natural to want to give our children the benefit of the doubt—and also to ensure we have a strong case!—confronting your child about drug use does not require the kind of evidence you might want to have.

Be in regular communication with your child and trust your gut.

As a parent, it's your responsibility to facilitate healthy conversations within your family. So let's look next at some tools you can use to set the stage for good conversations.

CHAPTER 13

Learning to Hold Space and Listen Well

Samuel and a few of his buddies from the football team, all older than him, were sleeping over at Matt's house. After Matt's parents went to sleep, the boys slipped out and walked to a nearby park, where Matt pulled some joints out of his jacket pocket and lit one up.

Samuel hadn't anticipated this and didn't want to smoke pot. But in the situation in which he found himself, he didn't have the courage or conviction to decline. As the boys shared the joints, Samuel started to feel relaxed in ways that he usually wasn't. As they were heading back to the house, Matt discovered one extra joint in his pocket. Since Samuel had been the only "first-timer" smoking that night, Matt gave it to him. Although he didn't really anticipate smoking it alone, Samuel thanked Matt and shoved it in his pocket.

When Samuel's mom was doing laundry a few days later, emptying pockets of coins and receipts, she came across the joint.

She could have responded in any number of ways.

She might have thrown open Samuel's bedroom door, held up the joint, and announced, "Grounded for six weeks!" and then slammed the door in a rage.

Or she might have suddenly become very anxious, fearful for her son's future. At the dinner table that night, she might have brought up the article she'd just read about a boy who'd used marijuana and then crashed a car.

She also might have looped in Samuel's dad so that they could all sit down together to talk later that evening. If the talk was what we're calling "old school," Samuel's parents would both bark and yell and shame and send him away to his room.

But there's another option that includes getting curious (listening), holding space, and validating.

Samuel's mother might have gently queried, "Hey, bud, what's going on?"

His father might have begun, "Son, I'm curious what's happening in your life. Can you share with us?"

And ideally, after opening the door, Samuel's parents would listen well and make room or "hold space" for him to share honestly.

And then they might validate Samuel's experience. While an "old school" response would be to reject his experience, ignore his feelings, and judge him, the parent who "validates" is interested in learning about and understanding the child's emotional experience. To be clear, "validating" is different than "endorsing."

For example, if Samuel's parents listen well to him, they might gain a deeper understanding of how tricky it could have felt to be in his shoes. One of them might say, "Boy, I see what you mean. That feels like a pretty hard choice to make."

They're not endorsing the use of marijuana, but when they listen, hold space, and validate what Samuel experienced—as a ninth grader wanting to be accepted by upperclassmen—their child experiences the compassion his parents have for him.

Old School, New School

Some of us who are parenting today were raised in homes with parents who were interested in listening to us and understanding us. Others of us, though, were raised in homes with parents whose loud mantra was, "I said it! That settles it. The end." We're going to call that "old school." And those parents were likely doing all they knew how to do.

But today, we're encouraging parents to take a real interest in their children so they can understand why their children might be acting out.

The "why" matters.

Emily Cox, who serves adolescents and families as a therapist in Raleigh, North Carolina, notes that spending time "wondering" can be useful for parents. She suggests asking:

- Why might my child be using marijuana?
- Why and how was my child introduced to marijuana?
- Why is my child attracted to marijuana?
- Why is marijuana use problematic for my child?

If you're married, you can have this wondering conversation with your spouse. If you're not married but co-parent well together, invite your child's other parent into this wondering conversation. And if you're parenting solo, use a journal to reflect on the "whys" that might be operating in your child's heart.

Be Present by Holding Space

"Holding space" is about being completely present for someone else to support them. When you "hold space," you literally *make room* for another. When you hold space, it's not about you as the listener. It's about the other. It's about being with someone in loving support so that they feel seen, heard, known, and loved. It's what each of us wants for ourselves and our children.

As you purpose to hold space in conversation with your child, you must:

1. Listen well
2. Make room for feelings
3. Remember that it's not about you. It's 100 percent about your child
4. Stay present. Avoid the temptation to minimize or problem-solve
5. Refrain from judgment

Listen Well

Too often, when someone is sharing with us, we can get tangled up with thoughts of how we'll respond and what we'll say next. Really good listening, though, is when we listen to understand what the person is sharing.

When we practice active listening, we let the person express all that they want to share and then we repeat back what we heard them say. If there's a part we got wrong, they can correct us.

Allow Room for Feelings

The person who is sharing something meaningful with you is likely holding some feelings about his or her situation. If your child has been caught using marijuana, he might be feeling shame or guilt. He might feel afraid of what the consequences of his actions will be. He might feel sad for no observable reason at all. Pay attention to what the other person might be feeling.

Let It Be about Your Child

When we hold space for others, it needs to be about them and not about us. Because we're naturally self-referenced, it can be tempting to center ourselves. We might do that by being distracted by thoughts of what others at church will think of our family. Or we might drift off on a mental tangent. Even when we want to chime in about our experiences, it's more valuable to stay focused on what your child is saying.

Stay Present

When we feel uncomfortable with the feelings or vulnerability of another, we can be tempted to "leave" rather than stay present mentally and emotionally. Even if we don't move physically, we can be tempted to flee the feelings that another's sharing evokes in us.

It can be tempting to try to solve "the problem." Or we might try to minimize what the other person may be feeling. Those are both ways of "leaving" the other person when we feel anxious or powerless to help. Trust that what is most helpful will not be your clever solutions or minimizing the other person's experience.

Refrain from Judgment

Here's the thing: An essential component of holding space for another person is the importance of refraining from judgment. As the listener, we create a safe space where the person sharing can be received as he or she is.

Engaging with our children while refraining from judgment can be tough for a lot of parents, especially Christian parents. We fear that if we don't make our judgment of our children's poor choices plain, somehow we will be endorsing their activities. If you feel that way, know that it's natural. It is difficult to be fully present to our children while refraining from judgment. Yet this is what our children need.

When we fail to hold this safe space for our children, they may think they must distance themselves from us to feel safe. Yet when we purpose to hold space for our children and allow them to be as they are in that space, they learn that it's safe to draw near to us.

One More Word about Not Judging

Although one of the most-quoted Bible verses—as much as or more by non-Christians than by Christians!—is "judge not lest ye be judged," sometimes "not judging" is easier said than done. Specifically, it can feel very counterintuitive for parents who want the best for their children. And that's why we want to underscore that this posture of holding space is what we experience when we are received by a gracious God. Although God is the One with the authority to judge, because of what Jesus has done, we have the security of drawing near to God where we are seen, heard, known, and loved. God "holds space" for us to be as we are.

Author and former priest Brennan Manning describes God's gracious love for us when we don't deserve it. He shares:

> Jesus Christ, this very moment comes right to your seat and says, "I have a word for you. I know your whole life story. I know every skeleton in your closet. I know every moment of sin, shame, dishonesty, and degraded love that has darkened your past. Right now I know your shallow faith, your feeble prayer life, your inconsistent discipleship. And my word is this: I dare you to trust that I love you just as you are, and not as you should be. Because you're never going to be as you should be."[1]

Isn't that kind of amazing? Because so many of us wrestle to accept God's radical, unconditional love for us, Manning paraphrases it plainly: "I love you just as you are, and not as you should be." That posture that Jesus offers us is exactly the posture with which we can speak with our children.

I love you as you are and not as you should be.

We naturally want to cushion our unconditional love with some conditions, some disclaimers, some judgments: "I love you, but I don't approve of your behavior." (While technically true, don't say it when you're holding space!) "I love you, but I am concerned for your safety." "I love you, but..."

Our children need to know that we love them as they are and not as they should be—nor as we wish they would be. Although it's counterintuitive, that kind of radical, unconditional love makes space for our children to make better choices.

Validate

Stacey Sadler, a therapist practicing in Missouri City, Texas, encourages parents to validate their children's experiences and feelings even when they do not agree with their behavior. Like practicing a non-judgmental presence with our children, this is another one that can be difficult for parents to execute.

Let's say your seventeen-year-old comes home from school and announces that he's getting a lion tattooed on his back. Your first reaction is to scream, "Noooooooo!" But you resist. Instead, you try to listen well. You ask your son why he wants to get a tattoo, and you listen to what he's telling you. You are curious about why he chose a lion. You pay attention to his answer. You inquire about where he might go to get this tattoo executed when he turns eighteen. And you are attentive as he describes a reputable tattoo parlor across town. When he's sharing, you listen well. You listen to *understand*, not to argue. When he's done, you're able to validate his desire to get a tattoo of a lion on his back and also validate that the thought of it makes him feel powerful. You have learned something about your son—that he wants to feel powerful—when you listened and validated.

Sadler told us, "When you validate the experiences and feelings behind what a child is saying, you have earned the right to be heard." What that means is that when a child's experiences have been heard, she is more willing to hear from you. Once you've listened well and validated your child's experiences and feelings, you can ask follow-up questions like this: "And what does that mean for…?" Or "Have you considered this other thing…?"

Does the conversation about the tattoo make you feel a little uncomfortable? Yes. But you can manage that.

Do you feel like you're betraying every parent everywhere if you don't shoot down his idea the moment it passes his lips? Of course.

But after our exchange, you notice that your child has opened up to you in new ways.

Sadler remarks, "We are afraid to have the tough conversations. We also fear that our children will equate our validation with approval. But when we are able to listen and seek understanding, even when we disagree, we can help our children navigate difficult decisions and situations with which they will be faced."

When we validate our children's experiences—even ones with which we disagree—and their feelings, we open the doors of relationship. And we actually increase the odds that later on, they'll accept our advice.

Because many of us grew up with parents who didn't listen well and who didn't validate our experiences and feelings, this may not come naturally to us. So Sadler offers a few examples of validating statements:

- "I see how that might be true."
- "That makes sense."
- "You are really feeling__________" (repeat what they've named).
- "I see you are upset."
- "Hmmm..."
- "Let me think about that."
- "I see you care a lot about that."
- "You might be right."

These types of statements keep the lines of communication open between you and your child.

We'll say it again: a lot of what we need to do to hold space, listen well, and validate feels *counterintuitive*! It can feel like we're *endorsing* behavior with which we disagree. But when you practice these proven communication skills, you aren't condoning your child's behavior. You're creating a space where your child can be seen, heard, known, and loved.

CHAPTER 14

Get Curious, Not Furious

Nona Jones is an author, speaker, pastor, and head of faith-based partnerships at Facebook.

In her book *Success from the Inside Out*, she shares about her difficult childhood and what God has done in her life. In a recent interview with UCB Media, she discussed her adolescence, saying, "My behavior literally deteriorated because I was experiencing so much chaos at home. So I was acting out at school and I was angry. Teachers just saw my behavior and assumed I was a bad kid. That I just had problems and I was just angry. What no one ever asked was, 'What happened to you to make you behave this way?'"[1]

No one ever asked.

Adolescents need adults who ask. Adolescents need adults who are curious. These adults are interested in more than what behaviors are happening; they're interested in *why* they're happening.

Can you imagine what might have been different if just one adult in Nona's life had engaged her with genuine interest to discover *why* she was acting out? It's what she most needed, and it's what our children also need.

That shift from "what" to "why" might not come naturally for you. When you can't let go of the "what," you're unlikely to be of much use to your children. But when you can get at the heart of the matter—quite literally noticing what is going on in the heart of your child—you will be in a better position to move forward together.

When you're curious, your posture is one of wondering, of investigation, of interest. If this kind of a posture toward your child feels foreign, know that it's a skill you can learn to use. It's like having a new tool in your toolbox that you can use today!

Maintain a Calm, Conversational Tone

You are responsible for setting the tone of the conversations you'll have with your children. When you're feeling angry, bitter, disappointed, or frustrated, you're making it more difficult for them to engage with you. When anyone feels demeaned, attacked, or judged, our natural response is to armor up! We naturally want to defend ourselves from what we perceive as a threat. And that's why it's so critical—and smart!—to use a calm, "matter-of-fact" tone in these conversations.

When the Apostle Paul was writing to the believers in Galatia, he could have been offering marching orders for twenty-first-century families dealing with marijuana use when he wrote, "But the Holy Spirit produces this kind of fruit in our lives: love, joy, peace, patience, kindness, goodness, faithfulness, gentleness, and self-control" (Galatians 5:22–23). Demonstrating the fruit of the Spirit anoints the conversations we have with our kids. When we bear these fruits, we open the lines of communication rather than close them.

This said, tricky conversations can trigger feelings in us that are the opposite of the fruitfulness we long to embody: lovelessness, despair, anxiety, impatience, unkindness, evil, betrayal, abruptness, and lack of restraint. And when we're bullied by these traitors, it's hard to stay curious.

If you've lost your cool, if you're rattled, if you're being bullied by your own feelings, take a break. You lose nothing by pausing to gather your composure.

"I'm going to take a break for a few minutes. You take a break, too. And we'll get back together in ten minutes."

"I need to go to the restroom. I'll be right back."

"Why don't we grab a snack and then regroup in a few minutes."

A few signs will signal to you that you might need to take a break:

- You physically feel your blood pressure rising or your heart racing
- You hear the pitch of your voice rising
- You hear the volume of your voice rising
- Your feelings interfere with your ability to be present with your child
- Your thoughts interfere with your ability to be present with your child

The vibe you want to embody as you converse with your child is love, joy, peace, forbearance, kindness, goodness, faithfulness, gentleness, and self-control.

Prepare yourself as you need to in order to get your head in this space.

Take a Genuine Interest in Your Child and Her Experiences

When you first held that little bundle of joy in your arms, you likely wondered who he or she would become. Over the years, you found out. You discovered what her temperament was like. You knew something about how she related to others. You learned whether she was physically coordinated and oriented toward outdoor sports and whether she was intellectually curious.

That act of discovering who your child is truly is an ongoing process. You have no way to know your child as a teenager until he or she is a teenager! So the more interest you have in knowing who your child is, the better. And another benefit to your taking a genuine interest in who your children are is that your interactions help them to become aware of who they are as well.

Whether you found a beer can hidden in your child's bedroom or whether he's calling you from jail, a curious approach to conversation *opens* lines of communication rather than closing them.

The goal of conversation with your child is to discover more about her, as well as her experiences. You're not focusing on the "what"; you're discovering the "why." When you get curious, you're wondering:

- What is my child thinking?
- What is motivating her?
- Where did this go sideways?

Remember, this is about your child and not you. It's easy to get distracted by our own thoughts and feelings, but this moment is about discovering more about who your child is.

It can help to notice your body during these conversations. Are you clenching your teeth? Squeezing your hands into fists? Crossing your arms? Furrowing your brow? Consider being very intentional with your body posture as you engage with your child. Be turned toward her. Open your arms. Relax your hands. Communicate openness on your face. Let your child see someone who is eager to know, understand, and love her.

Gather Information

When you decide to get curious and not furious, you approach the situation almost like an investigator. But don't act like a cop! Don't interrogate your child by pummeling him with endless questions that can feel like a barrage of Nerf gun bullets. Instead, assume the posture of someone more like the new youth group leader who is genuinely eager to learn who your child is.

"I'm wondering how you were able to get that beer..."

And then listen well.

"I'm interested in knowing more about how your evening unfolded last night..."

And then listen well.

"I'd like to discover why that's important to you..."

And then listen well.

Ask your questions well. "I'm wondering how you were able to get that beer" is likely going to be more effective than "How the h*#% did you get the booze?!?" "I'm interested in knowing more..." is likely going to be more effective than "What the [bleep] did you do?" And "I'd like to discover..." is likely going to be more effective than "You're just like your brother! What were you thinking?"

Ask your questions well and then listen well.

Measure Your Response

When your child does open up to share information with you, she will be evaluating how you respond. The way you respond signals whether it's safe for her to be honest or whether it's in her self-interest to keep her mouth shut. If you scowl, turn away, shame, or rage, the conversation is likely to be a short one! But if your child senses that she is accepted and loved regardless of her behavior, she is likely to be willing to share more with you.

Here are some responses that let your child know you're receiving the information she's sharing:

- Eye contact
- Relaxed face and body
- A gentle nod
- A follow-up question for clarification
- Summarizing what you've heard to ensure you're understanding correctly

We know that these might feel like a lot of new skills to be juggling as you care for your child. And you likely won't nail all of them right away. Just as you are practicing being gentle with your child, be gentle with yourself as well. If you recognize that you've missed the mark—by raising your voice or saying something you wish you hadn't—pause to let your child know you're sorry and want to do better.

When you choose not to get furious but to get curious, you love your child well.

CHAPTER 15

How to Have the Conversation

Parents, you are not alone. A lot of us are facing some of the same challenges. We find ourselves in situations we could not have predicted when our children were in diapers:

- "I'm noticing marijuana smoke is wafting through my HVAC system and into my bedroom."
- "I know this joker who just got dragged to the vice principal's office did *not* just say 'It's not mine' and 'I'm holding it for a friend.'"
- "Hmmmm…why does my kid have a prescription medication bottle with his friend's name on it, and why is it filled with dried green leaves?"
- "After I just spent twenty bucks on a marijuana test at the drugstore, this li'l dummy just pretended

to urinate and then handed me a cup of urine to test that is *cold*?"

- "Although I'm on a work trip on the other side of the country, I'm watching my fancy video doorbell as one of my children puts tape over the camera so that I cannot see whatever hooligans are about to parade in and out of the dwelling where I pay the mortgage."

We never could have predicted these kinds of shenanigans, and there's certainly no script for how to handle them.

How does a thoughtful, well-resourced Christian parent respond to the kind of situation that can make some of our minds go blank?

The big win for these kinds of conversations is when parents and children are working together toward a solution. As the adult, your job is to set the stage for that to happen. Learn as much as you can, decide how you'll proceed, and then do what you said you'd do.

Be Emotionally Grounded

When we discover that our child has been using marijuana, it's pretty normal for us to experience all kinds of feelings. Anger—or rage—is a popular one for a lot of us. Fear is another. Sadness, too. Or we might even feel shame—"Are we *that* kind of family?"—about our child's choices.

The most important thing you can do when engaging with your child is to remain calm, measured, mature, and in your right mind. Steve says, "We want to restrain ourselves. Be the adult in the room. Realize that this is about the child and not about us."

And there it is.

The conversation ceases to be about your child when you make it about you. Whether you say these words aloud or merely think them in your head, making it about you might sound something like…

I raised you better than this.

I'm so disappointed.

I'm so angry.

I feel insulted.

I'm hurt that she's separating from me.

What did I do wrong?

I didn't know he was rebelling like this.

What will people think of my child?

What will people think of me?

I'm hurt I didn't know about this.

When we center ourselves, we fail our children. And while it's natural to have some of these thoughts, we can also choose to release our own self-interest for a moment to be present to our child. So man up, woman up, and let the interaction be about understanding and loving your child.

Be Curious

As we discussed in the previous chapter, Steve suggests that parents should get curious, not furious. If you've centered yourself, if you've released the "furious," you're on your way. Great first step. And then "get curious."

When you're talking to your kids about marijuana, "curious" might sound like:

"So tell me about your relationship with marijuana..."

You're calm. You're rational. You're not accusing. You're taking an interest. During this part of the conversation, you're gathering as much information as you can. And ideally, you're engaging with a very calm manner, open posture, and even tone. Because you were not born yesterday, you know that whatever your child says next might be the truth—and it might not be. Regardless, stay calm. Continue to gather more information.

"Who are the folks that you like to do this with?"

"Where do you get this stuff?"

"Where do you get the money to do this?"

Were you to close your eyes and imagine two parents asking the same question, you could probably hear it spoken in two very different tones. One parent (not you, of course) might conduct his judicial investigation with a harsh, angry tone:

"So, who are you smoking with, anyway? I'll bet it's Blake. I never liked that kid. And where are you getting it? Because I will murder whoever sold this to you. And how do you pay for it? Stealing? Using the allowance *I gave you*? Whatever your answer is, I'm going to use it to destroy you."

To be clear, that's the kind of tone you want to avoid.

Another parent (maybe you) invites conversation by using a calm, even, curious, and interested tone: "I'm curious who you end up smoking with. And I can't even imagine where it comes from. Where do you get it? How do you pay for it?"

The big idea is to use language, tone, facial expression, and body language to open up the lines of communication, welcoming real dialogue.

It's useful to remember that your child might be barraged by his or her own feelings in this situation:

- He might be *surprised* that you know
- She might feel *ashamed* you found out
- He might be *angry* a sibling snitched

- She might feel *guilty* for transgressing her own values
- He might feel *sad* because he let you down
- She might be *afraid* of the consequences

Knowing that your child is experiencing a whole range of emotions can give you compassion and understanding that he or she might be feeling stuck as you process the situation together. If your child isn't quick to answer, give her some space. Make some room. Practice patience. Encourage him to share. The vibe you create in the room is going to signal to your child whether it's a safe place to share honestly.

What If I Can't Stay Calm? What If I Get Furious?

For a lot of us, navigating these kinds of conversations without being consumed with anger, fear, sadness, guilt, or shame is new. If you feel rattled or overwhelmed, remember to take a break.

"Let's take a break and get back together in ten minutes."

Steve suggests having a talk with yourself in the bathroom mirror:

"I can do this."

"I can be the adult in the room."

"I have the maturity and resources to facilitate a good conversation."

"I'm going to get curious and listen well."

Beloved friend, you can do this.

What If My Child Stays Silent?

If that is the case, Steve suggests saying, "If you're willing to talk about this, there are lots of options for us."

When he or she chooses to engage in the discussion, possibilities become available that aren't options if he or she won't speak. This empowers your child.

But what if your child is more belligerently silent? For a variety of reasons, he or she might choose not to engage in honest conversation with you. In situations like these, Steve suggests saying:

"If you're not willing to talk about it with us, your parents, then you may find yourself in treatment talking to a drug and alcohol counselor."

You likely won't need to mention drug treatment in the first few minutes of information-gathering. But if you eventually feel like you're up against a brick wall, it's just one more tool to have in the toolbox.

What If My Child Lies?

If he feels like he's backed into a corner, your child might be tempted to lie. Or fudge a little. Or twist the truth. When you notice or suspect that your child is lying, take a breath and recalibrate. You don't have to spend a lot of time and energy sussing out and prosecuting the lie. If you stay there, the conversation stays stuck.

It might be useful to deal with a lie the way you deal with silence.

"If you're not willing to talk honestly about it with us, your parents, then you may find yourself in treatment talking to a drug and alcohol counselor."

"If you're willing to talk honestly about it, there are lots of options for us."

Just as in the rest of your conversation, keep the tone of your voice neutral. You're not trying to scare your child with threats. You are matter-of-factly reporting that if Plan A of discussing the situation as a family doesn't work out, there are other options.

Take Time to Process

Some parents don't feel like they're good on their feet and would prefer to have time to prepare a script. They might feel flustered or overwhelmed in the moment. If you're one of them, Steve suggests wrapping up your information-gathering conversation with your child by saying something like this:

"All right, let me think about this. We'll talk again tomorrow."

You are not obliged to announce every thought and feeling you're having. Nor do you have to announce a final, definitive system of consequences.

And, as Steve points out, "It gives them an opportunity to worry a bit." It also gives them the breathing room they might need to make the best decision they can. Just as you might need time and space to think clearly, your child can benefit from the same opportunity.

What Next?

Let's say you've had a discussion with your child about marijuana. Maybe you spread it out over a few days. Ideally, it was a mutual conversation where you were both able to share and listen. Here's a way to transition to what comes next:

"We're going to give you five days to figure out how you're never going to do this again while you're living with us."

It places responsibility for action squarely where it belongs—with your child.

It gives him or her time to reflect and plan.

It gives your child the opportunity to make a good decision.

In the best of all possible worlds, you reconvene after five days, and your child offers a satisfactory action plan. Maybe she decides to stop spending time with a particular friend. Maybe she breaks up with the boyfriend with whom she smoked. Or she might choose to tell her friends that she got busted and won't be smoking because she can't get busted again. Ideally, your child will take responsibility for solving the problem.

If your child doesn't offer a reasonable plan of action, you might need to remind her of what's next.

"Using marijuana is just not an option for you until you're out of this house. If this is such a big part of your life that you can't figure out how not to do it, we'll have to get you some help."

There's no reason for these conversations to be overly emotional, dramatic, or confrontational. Use a peaceful tone and offer the options calmly and clearly.

After the Reckoning

When your child has made a commitment to live without using marijuana, he or she will either succeed or fail. Although you have no control over your child's choices, you do have control over how you will respond.

When She Succeeds

When Steve's daughter graduated from high school without having used alcohol or drugs, he made good on his promise and bought her a car. She was rewarded for consistently making life-giving decisions.

Even if you can't afford a car, you might make other rewards contingent on your child doing well in school and avoiding certain behaviors. Maybe it's the privilege of borrowing the family car. Or you'll cover the cost of his car insurance. It might be that you'll help as much as you can with higher education. Or it might be the privilege of living at home between college semesters.

As parents, you choose the privileges or rewards your child can enjoy when he or she chooses to be free of marijuana use.

When She Fails

Maybe your child talked a good game about quitting marijuana, but—by weakness or by willful choice—she decided to use again. This is when the privileges end.

"We were hoping that the risk of these consequences would be painful enough for you to stop using, but that didn't happen. Now, because of your choices, you've lost the privilege of living here."

If you're soft-hearted, you likely began scrolling through excuses and exceptions when you read those words. If you're not a cold-hearted villain, it takes courage to implement the consequences you've outlined. But we want you to hear that it's possible. Not only is it possible, but it is the loving thing for your child.

She will likely find a friend's place to crash. Or you may allow her to pitch a tent in your driveway. If your child's marijuana use has gotten this far, it's incumbent upon you to implement the consequences you originally offered.

"This thing is so important to you that you chose to forfeit the security of a roof over your head, food on the table, transportation, relationship with your family, and even an education. That means it's really, really important to you. And when something is that important to you and is causing you to make foolish decisions, it needs to be eliminated."

If your child admits that marijuana is harming her life but that she can't seem to stop, it's time for treatment.

You Can Do This

You might feel anxious about whether or not you can do this.

You can.

And when you do—when you have these conversations, when you welcome your child to make better choices, when you execute the consequences you said you would—you are going to be so proud of yourself. It's going to make you happy! And when you have the courage to begin, you'll find yourself doing it more and more often.

You can do this.

You can be the adult in the room.

You can facilitate a good conversation.

You can listen well.

You can follow through with the consequences you stated.

You've got this.

CHAPTER 16

Engage and Stay Engaged

"Hey guys, here's some lemonade and warm chocolate chip cookies," Charlene said as she pushed through the screen door on to the front porch, trying to balance paper cups and napkins.

Her son Colin was visiting with his friend Randal. Randal had graduated from another high school in town the previous year, and the boys had been introduced by mutual friends. Randal, whose parents had bought him a Mercedes-Benz convertible for his sixteenth birthday, was taking classes at a local junior college. Colin was just a high school sophomore. As the boys got to know one another, Charlene had been investing time and energy into getting to know Randal, as well, and letting him know that she cared about him.

A few days earlier, Colin's sister Jamie had shown Charlene a photograph Randal had posted on Instagram. He and Colin were at a nearby park, and the cryptic language he used signaled that they were getting high. In tandem with some situations shared by other parents, Charlene felt reasonably certain that Randal was using and dealing marijuana.

Pulling up a chair next to the boys, ready to address them both, Charlene began, "Colin, I'm sorry I'm going to embarrass you…"

Colin, sinking into his chair, did nothing to hide his mortification.

"…but you're still in high school. Randal, not only are you not in high school, but you're also over eighteen. I know you have access to drugs, and I need you to hear that you can be held accountable by law. You can even do jail time."

Randal's eyes widened as he gulped his lemonade. Colin had pulled his hoodie over his face.

Charlene continued, "I don't know what you're hearing at home, but it's time for you to wake up. There are real-life consequences now, and you need to be careful."

Both boys were stunned.

"And you," she said, turning to Colin, "need to be sure you don't screw up the rest of high school. You boys need to realize that this is just a blip in your life. You can't screw it up just to have some fun with your crew. It doesn't pay. There's so much more for you in life: college experiences, work experiences, so many more friends."

The boys kept listening.

Turning to Randal, Charlene said, "I don't know you well, but you've got some power because you have access to stuff people want."

Randal didn't disagree.

"How would you feel," she asked, "if you hurt one of these kids?"

Randal looked down at the porch steps.

"Randal, I just think you have so much potential, and I only want good things for you. You were made for more than this."

Both Colin and Randal stayed silent. Glancing at Colin, Charlene could tell he was miffed—which she'd expected.

After a few minutes, Randal looked up at Charlene and spoke.

"Thank you," he said. "No one has ever talked to me like that before."

Putting her hand on his back, Charlene said, "You're welcome. You can have a bright future. That's what I want for you."

Over the following weeks and months, Charlene continued to get to know Randal and care for him. When it would have been easier to disengage, she stayed engaged.

Initiate Conversations with Your Child about Marijuana

We encourage you to talk to your child about marijuana. While it might feel counterintuitive to introduce the subject of illicit drugs to your family, it's actually exactly what your child most needs. The American Academy of Child and Adolescent Psychiatry (AACAP) confirms that talking to your child at an early age about marijuana will benefit him later on. Specifically, they suggest talking to your child when he is in late elementary or early middle school. When your child knows that you're open to talking about marijuana—and even that you might know something about it!—you lay the groundwork for him to be able to come to you later.

If you've missed the late-elementary/early-middle-school window, the best time to begin talking about marijuana use with your child is *today.* While we wish we could offer you a script, we realize that every conversation about marijuana will likely be different. The conversation you have will depend on your child's age and maturity, whether or not she's used marijuana, who her friends are, and several other factors. What we know for sure is that initiating these conversations will benefit your child.

While you can be prepared to discuss marijuana use with your child, you can't predict exactly how that conversation will go. If your teen or young adult child calls you from jail because he's been arrested for selling marijuana to minors, you can expect to have a different conversation than if the same young person comes home smelling like marijuana smoke. And the conversation you have with the child who is texting with his friend about the possibility of consuming edibles at a sleepover will be different than the conversation you'll have with the young person who is waking up screaming from marijuana-induced nightmares. Your job is to do what you have to do when you have to do it.

What's most critical is that you engage and stay engaged. Is it more comfortable to avoid these conversations? Absolutely. And is it more comfortable to have deliberate conversations with your child than to receive a call from jail informing you that he's been using and selling marijuana? Of course. Do what you have to do—today.

If your parents didn't have frank, open conversations with you about alcohol, drugs, or sex, it's likely that initiating these conversations with your own children will feel foreign at first. We understand, and it's why we're offering you the tools you need to navigate these discussions. While they'll naturally feel unfamiliar at first, they get easier. We promise.

The AACAP offers these five tips for the conversations you'll have with your children about marijuana use:[1]

- Ask what they have heard about using marijuana. Listen carefully, pay attention, and try not to interrupt. Avoid making negative or angry comments.
- Offer your child facts about the risks and consequences of smoking marijuana.
- Ask your child to give examples of the effects of marijuana. This will help you make sure that your child understands what you talked about.
- If you choose to talk to your child about your own experiences with drugs, be honest about why you used and the pressures that contributed to it. Be careful not to minimize the dangers of marijuana or other drugs and be open about any negative experiences you may have had. Given how much stronger marijuana is today, its effect on your child would likely be much different than what you experienced.

- Explain that research tells us that the brain continues to mature into the twenties. While it is developing, there is greater risk of harm from marijuana use.

When you discover that your child has used marijuana, we want you to be prepared to have a fruitful conversation and take the action needed to help him. When you can have this conversation calmly—without anxiety, rage, or despair—you help your child hear and learn from the natural consequences of choosing to use marijuana.

Plan to Have More Than One Conversation

When some of us were growing up, we may have gotten "the talk" about sex as we approached adolescence. Our parents might have shooed our siblings away, sat us down alone in the living room, taken a somber tone, and proceeded to mortify us by informing us about the birds and the bees. (Hint: if they actually called it "the birds and the bees" rather than using more accurate language for human sexuality, we were probably doomed already.) But what many of us have discovered in our own parenting, however, is that one talk might not be enough.

When we introduce a topic that can be tricky—whether it's about drugs, or sex, or even something as benign as adoption—and continue to communicate about it to our children over time, we signal to them that this is something our family discusses. They take their cues from us, and when we discuss the topic, it shows them that it's not taboo. It's not off limits. We model comfort in discussing it, so they can be comfortable too.

The fact is that our children need for us to introduce topics like these many times over many years. At the age of ten, a child can understand some of what we introduce when we discuss marijuana use. At the age of thirteen, she'll be able to understand and process a bit more, and by the time she's seventeen, she'll have the capacity to understand even more about its consequences and risks.

Parent, we know it's hard. It's easier to throw up a prayer to God, squint your eyes shut, and hope for the best. But we are convinced that being vigilant by engaging the issue and pursuing conversations with your child is the most courageous and loving way to parent.

CHAPTER 17

How Not to Communicate with Your Child

We mentioned that studies show young people are less susceptible to experimenting with drugs and alcohol when parents communicate well about their use and abuse. Check.

But notice that we didn't say the likelihood of *experimentation* decreases when parents simply communicate. Not all forms of communication are created equal. Here are some danger zones to avoid when you speak with your children about marijuana.

Parents Do All the Talking

You know the stereotype of the parent who blathers on and on and on while a teen just rolls his eyes and checks out of the conversation? It's a stereotype for a reason!

When a child doesn't engage, frustrated parents are often tempted to fill the space with their own words. But there is a better way!

We know that kids learn best when they talk, not when the only audible voice belongs to a parent. We encourage you to use creative strategies to engage your child in the conversation at hand.

- We'd love to hear your thoughts on that…
- I wonder why that happened…
- If I was in that situation, I think I'd feel_____. How about you?
- We'd love to hear more…

Your conversation will be more fruitful—and be an actual conversation instead of a monologue—when you find gentle, creative ways to help your child engage.

Parents Are Bleeding Big Feelings

Kids are most likely to open up when adults are able to engage with a non-anxious presence. You might think about this as feeling firmly rooted and grounded when you're relating to your child. You're operating out of a mature and emotionally healthy place and are not being bossed around by your feelings.

You may *feel* anxious about your child's future. You might even have legitimate fears about where your child is headed. This is normal. But when you're not able to contain those feelings while talking to your child, he or she senses your anxiety.

Or maybe you're furious that your child offered marijuana to his younger sibling, livid that his choices got him kicked off the baseball team, or angry that he used his last few dollars on pot instead of getting a Christmas gift for his sister. This is also normal. But when your anger leaks out as rage, your child can't help but notice.

It might be that you're feeling sad. Maybe you've seen other loved ones become addicted to substances, and you're sad that your child is making similar choices. Or you might be feeling low or experiencing depression, for this or countless other reasons. When you feel burdened by sadness, your child notices.

But there is an alternative to being untethered, ungrounded, or unhinged. You don't have to be bullied by your feelings. When you're able to set them aside for a moment, you can be rooted in a more solid place. You can listen well. You can be present during the conversation. It may take some practice, but you will be better able to parent your child when you are able to exercise a calm, non-anxious presence.

Parents Get Loud and Overreact

When we feel passionately about something, it's easy for our emotions to bubble, the pitch of our voice to rise, and the volume to escalate. But these things also make it difficult to keep the lines of communication open. You and your teen will communicate best when you can speak with a reasonable volume and a calm, measured tone of voice.

The Parent Shames the Child

"Loser."

"Failure."

"Pathetic."

"Screwup."

As parents, we harm our children when we speak shaming words about who they are.

I think that one of the most important things we can do for our children is to hold in our hearts and minds a vision of the people God made them to be.

Several years ago, Tom's wife left him, and his life and business fell to pieces. Retreating from everything and everyone, he moved to a new city, rented an apartment, and started drinking heavily. Although he didn't pick up his phone when people who loved him called, one faithful friend persisted. He eventually flew across the country and showed up at Tom's apartment to find all the curtains drawn, a disheveled environment, and a struggling drunken friend consumed by darkness.

Looking Tom in the eye, the friend said simply, "This isn't who you are."

We must do the same for our children. When we look at them, we must remember that their poor choices are not who they are. And we must hold up the vision of the young woman or young man God created them to be.

The Parent Ignores or Minimizes the Problem

It is easier to ignore the fact that a child is using marijuana than to confront it. We might do this because we minimize the fact that it is problematic on several levels. We might do it because we don't have the support of a partner to help us face it. We might do it because we are in denial, and we'd prefer to pretend that our child is other than she is. We might do it because facing it would mean we'd have to face some of our own unhealthy behaviors. We might do it because we don't want to risk rupturing the relationship we have with our child. Or we might do it because we're just tired, and ignoring it is easier. Yet when we ignore our child's marijuana use, we do her a disservice, and we fail to love her well.

If this is you, talk to someone who can support you as you support your child.

The Child Directs the Conversation

"It's not even very bad."

"It's legal in this state."

"I hardly ever do it."

"But let's talk about Jason and the totally worse stuff he is doing…"

Although you've committed to not lecturing or doing all the talking, it's still important for you to be the person who is facilitating the conversation.

If your child goes off on a tangent during your conversation, you need to redirect the conversation to keep it on track. What matters most in your conversation is whether your child is going to stop using marijuana on his own or whether other forces will be brought to bear on the problem.

You serve your child well when you facilitate a conversation that stays on track.

The Child Lies

It can feel pretty frustrating when our children lie to us. Whether we catch them and call them out on it in the moment or do some follow-up research to discover they've lied, it can be maddening.

But that's not useful to you or to your child. No one benefits. Instead, it's actually more helpful to admit to yourself that you don't have the ability to change his choices. And when your child is lying, you're not able to have the kind of dialogue you need to reach a solution.

If lies have stymied your conversation, Steve suggests saying something like, "If we can't be a bit more honest with each other, this isn't going to work. And if this doesn't work, then we'll have to get some professional help for you and for our family."

If your child is lying, take a break. Let your child think it over. Regroup.

CHAPTER 18

We're Cheering You On

Parent,

Understanding and loving your child who uses marijuana requires love, attention, wisdom, and commitment. The fact that you are holding this book signals that you're taking the issue seriously and want to find the best ways to help your child.

You're not alone. As marijuana use becomes increasingly prevalent, more and more families are being impacted. If you feel shame that your child has gotten into trouble with marijuana, we understand. But you don't need to carry that shame. Many of us feel that whatever our children experience is our fault, but that's often not the case. (Now, if you smoke crack at home and buy liquor for your teens, it *might* be your fault.)

Many kids who have been loved well still experiment with marijuana. Be gentle with yourself if you feel like you haven't parented your child perfectly. None of us has.

While you can't control your child's behavior, your loving attention to the problem and consistent engagement can help your child find freedom from marijuana.

You can do this.

Notes

Chapter 3: What You Need to Know about Marijuana

1. "How Many Teens Use Marijuana?" National Institute on Drug Abuse, https://teens.drugabuse.gov/drug-facts/marijuana#topic-7.
2. "Monitoring the Future Study: Trends in Prevalence of Various Drugs," National Institute on Drug Abuse, December 17, 2020, https://www.drugabuse.gov/drug-topics/trends-statistics/monitoring-future/monitoring-future-study-trends-in-prevalence-various-drugs.
3. "War on Drugs," History.com, updated December 17, 2019, https://www.history.com/topics/crime/the-war-on-drugs.
4. Jeff Desjardins, "The 6,000-Year History of Medical Cannabis," Visual Capitalist, June 20, 2018, http://www.visualcapitalist.com/history-medical-cannabis-shown-one-giant-map.

5. Mary Barna Bridgeman and Daniel T. Abazia, "Medicinal Cannabis: History, Pharmacology, and Implications for the Acute Care Setting," *P&T* 42, no. 3 (March 2017): 180–88, https://www.ncbi.nlm.nih.gov/pmc/articles/PMC5312634.
6. "Frequently Asked Questions: Medical Marijuana Program," New York State Department of Health, updated November 2020, https://www.health.ny.gov/regulations/medical_marijuana/faq.htm.
7. "Opioid Addiction Being Treated with Medical Marijuana in Massachusetts," Partnership to End Addiction, October 2015, https://drugfree.org/drug-and-alcohol-news/opioid-addiction-treated-medical-marijuana-massachusetts.

Chapter 4: Questions Parents Ask about Marijuana

1. Jason Patel and Raman Marwaha, "Cannabis Use Disorder," StatPearls, updated November 29, 2020, https://www.ncbi.nlm.nih.gov/books/NBK538131.
2. Ken C. Winters and Chih-Yuan S. Lee, "Likelihood of Developing an Alcohol and Cannabis Use Disorder during Youth: Association with Recent Use and Age," *Drug Alcohol Dependence* 92, no. 1–3 (January 1, 2008): 239–47, doi.org/10.1016/j.drugalcdep.2007.08.005.
3. Deborah S. Hasin, Charles P. O'Brien, Marc Auriacombe et al., "DSM-5 Criteria for Substance Use Disorders: Recommendations and Rationale," *American Journal of Psychiatry* 170, no. 8 (August 2013): 834–51, doi:10.1176/appi.ajp.2013.12060782.

4. "Schizophrenia, Cannabis Use, and Alcohol Abuse Are Just Several Disorders That Are Related to Accelerated Brain Aging," Amen Clinics, August 21, 2018, https://www.amenclinics.com/blog/largest-brain-study-of-62454-scans-identifies-drivers-of-brain-aging.
5. "U.S. Surgeon General's Advisory: Marijuana Use and the Developing Brain," U.S. Department of Health and Human Services, Office of the Surgeon General, August 29, 2019, https://www.hhs.gov/surgeongeneral/reports-and-publications/addiction-and-substance-misuse/advisory-on-marijuana-use-and-developing-brain/index.html.
6. O. J. Kalant, "Report of the Indian Hemp Drugs Commission, 1893–94: A Critical Review," *International Journal of the Addictions* 7, no. 1 (1972): 77–96, doi.org/10.3109/10826087209026763.
7. Nora D. Volkow, James M. Swanson, A. Eden Evins et al., "Effects of Cannabis Use on Human Behavior, Including Cognition, Motivation, and Psychosis: A Review," *JAMA Psychiatry* 73, no. 3 (2016): 292–97, doi.org/10.1001/jamapsychiatry.2015.3278.
8. Maria Cheng, "Smoking Strong Pot Daily Raises Psychosis Risk, Study Finds," Associated Press, March 19, 2019, https://apnews.com/4f9b18c6ac0d4cd5a8c5ab85157ce190.
9. Malcolm Gladwell, "Is Marijuana as Safe as We Think?," *New Yorker*, January 14, 2019, https://www.newyorker.com/magazine/2019/01/14/is-marijuana-as-safe-as-we-think.

10. Brian Handwerk, “Modern Marijuana Is Often Laced with Heavy Metals and Fungus,” *Smithsonian Magazine*, March 23, 2015, https://www.smithsonianmag.com/science-nature/modern-marijuana-more-potent-often-laced-heavy-metals-and-fungus-180954696.
11. Zawn Villines, “How Long Can You Detect Marijuana in the Body?” Medical News Today, January 29, 2019, https://www.medicalnewstoday.com/articles/324315#marijuana-detection-windows.

Chapter 5: Marijuana and Family Dynamics

1. Stephen Arterburn and David Stoop, *Understanding and Loving a Person with Alcohol or Drug Addiction* (Colorado Springs, Colorado: David C. Cook, 2018).
2. Ibid.

Chapter 6: Start Making a Difference Today

1. D’vera Cohn and Jeffrey S. Passel, “A Record 64 Million Americans Live in Multigenerational Households,” Pew Research Center, Fact Tank, updated April 5, 2018, https://www.pewresearch.org/fact-tank/2018/04/05/a-record-64-million-americans-live-in-multigenerational-households/#:~:text=(Fewer%20than%20a%20million%20people,consisting%20of%20grandparents%20and%fire20grandchildren.

Chapter 7: Thinking through Family Policy

1. “The Average Cost of Marijuana by State,” Oxford Treatment Center, updated September 15, 2020, https://

www.oxfordtreatment.com/substance-abuse/marijuana/average-cost-of-marijuana.

2. Daniel G. Amen et al., "Discriminative Properties of Hippocampal Hypoperfusion in Marijuana Users Compared to Healthy Controls: Implications for Marijuana Administration in Alzheimer's Dementia," *Journal of Alzheimer's Disease* 56, no. 1 (2017): 261–73, https://content.iospress.com/articles/journal-of-alzheimers-disease/jad160833.

Chapter 11: Is There a Problem?

1. Stephen Arterburn and Jim Burns, *How to Talk to Your Kids about Drugs* (Eugene, Oregon: Harvest House Publishers, 2007).
2. This list is also from *How to Talk to Your Kids about Drugs.*

Chapter 12: Learning to Talk to Your Child about Marijuana

1. "What You Need to Know About Marijuana Use in Teens," Centers for Disease Control and Prevention, April 13, 2017, https://www.cdc.gov/marijuana/factsheets/teens.htm; "Marijuana," National Institute on Drug Abuse, https://teens.drugabuse.gov/drug-facts/marijuana; Kirsten Weir, "Marijuana and the Developing Brain," American Psychological Association, November 2015, https://www.apa.org/monitor/2015/11/marijuana-brain; "Regular Marijuana Use by Teens Continues to Be a Concern," National Institutes of Health, December 19, 2012, https://www.nih.gov/news-events/

news-releases/regular-marijuana-use-teens-continues-be-concern.

Chapter 13: Learning to Hold Space and Listen Well

1. Toddsters5, "Brennan Manning live at Woodcrest," YouTube, May 30, 2007, https://youtu.be/pQi_IDV2bgM.

Chapter 14: Get Curious, Not Furious

1. United Christian Broadcasters,"This Is My Story: Nona Jones, UCB," YouTube, January 16, 2020, https://www.youtube.com/watch?v=1yakSqV9CHM.

Chapter 16: Engage and Stay Engaged

1. "Marijuana and Teens," American Academy of Child & Adolescent Psychiatry, updated October 2019, https://www.aacap.org/AACAP/Families_and_Youth/Facts_for_Families/FFF-Guide/Marijuana-and-Teens-106.aspx.